Leading Off:

19th Century Superstars Who Shaped Professional Baseball

Ray Scheetz

ISBN: 978-1-0784-8580-7

Cover Photo: Chicago and All-America World Tour Teams, *America's National Game*, pg. 254.

For BRS & AIS.

CONTENTS

PRE-GAME INTRODUCTION

"The whole history of baseball has the quality of mythology."
– Bernard Malamud.

The National Baseball Hall of Fame and Museum is located in Cooperstown, NY, because Cooperstown was the hometown of Abner Doubleday. According to legend, Doubleday created the modern rules of baseball and first played the game that is our national pastime in 1839. Recognition of Doubleday's key role in developing baseball ties the game into our national fabric as he was a Union general during the Civil War who both fired the first shots at Fort Sumter and played a key role in the Battle of Gettysburg. Cooperstown reminds us that our national pastime was delivered to us by a man who literally played a major role in saving our nation. The only problem is: the story of Abner Doubleday's involvement in developing the game of baseball simply isn't true.

What is true is that, while various bat and ball games can be traced back to the middle ages of Europe, baseball is a uniquely American game. While the earliest European settlers of what would become the United States began their colonization of the continent, their children transplanted the games of England, and for generations, the bat and ball games of the American colonies and their mother country would have been closely related to one another, being played in the schoolyards of both countries even as the American Revolution was creating a permanent separation between them. Even the Revolutionary soldiers themselves, attests George Ewing's 1778 Valley Forge journal, "Exercisd in the afternoon in the intervals playd at base [sic]." Baseball was already in its infancy, but it had not yet been christened as the national pastime. At the dawn of the next century, a generation of men, Abner Doubleday's generation, was born, and those men built the American game as they built the American character – not as an achievement by a single man in a fixed moment, but as an organic progression that mixed the best that America had to offer with a bit of serendipity to create a national pastime.

Years later, baseball's popularity and its penchant for inviting reminiscences and historical comparisons led to a search for the sport's origin. Following the realization that Abner Doubleday was at West Point rather than Cooperstown in 1839, and that he never claimed to having any role in baseball's origin, historians began generally credit the creation of the modern game of baseball to Alexander Cartwright, a bank clerk and volunteer firefighter who also played with the New York Knickerbocker Baseball Club during the 1840s. Cartwright is said to have completed an initial and unique set of rules for baseball in September 1845, and the Knickerbockers are credited with playing the first official game of baseball against a team of cricketers in 1846. While coincidental, this alleged origin for baseball's foundational rules is every bit as symbolically American as an origin connected to an American Civil War hero.

Washington Irving, in addition to serving as the U.S. minister to Spain in the early 1840s, is one of America's most important early authors. He wrote in the vernacular, consistently placing his stories within the United States, and he is generally credited with perfecting the American short story. Irving achieved his accomplishments by embracing a mythological tradition, by reaching out to incorporate the American narrative tradition while exhibiting unique aspects of American history ranging from references to Native Americans and pirate treasure in "The Devil and Tom Walker" to local narratives tied to the American Revolution, as in "The Legend of Sleepy Hollow." To complete the delivery of his American mythology, as he rose to popular fame, Irving created the narrative persona Diedrich Knickerbocker for his *A History of New York* and his legendary "Rip Van Winkle". Knickerbocker, a supposed young, eccentric Dutch American, quickly became synonymous with a resident of New York descended from the early Dutch population, and thus in the name of Alexander Cartwright's team, the New York Knickerbocker Baseball Club, there exists an implicit and fundamental tie to the origin of American literary identity.

Cartwright himself has further ties to American history, as he participated in the 1849 California Gold Rush and subsequently moved to Hawaii, where he was an advisor to the royal family, dying just six months before the Hawaiian monarchy was toppled by American citizens, as a result of their business interests, in 1893. But most significantly, in his 1938 induction to the Baseball Hall of Fame in Cooperstown, Cartwright was identified as the "Father of Modern Base Ball." However, in the Spring 2014 volume of Baseball Research Journal, Richard Hershberger took on the Cartwright baseball origin story, identifying it as a poorly founded myth. While it is not disputed that Alexander Cartwright played a significant role in baseball's early years, and while the New York Knickerbockers were one of the most prominent early baseball teams, and they may have strongly supported its spread nationwide as the work of Angus Macfarlane identifies that many Knickerbockers reconvened to play a significant role in San Francisco baseball by 1851, there is no conclusive evidence of baseball's Cartwright origin. Thus, the story must be treated skeptically, tempering Cartwright's role in creating baseball into one where he was a significant contributor rather than a lone inventor, and no single definitive explanation of baseball's inception survives to the present day. Nonetheless, there are elements of baseball's origins that intertwine the game with several other fundamental elements of American national identity.

Consistent in the various narratives of baseball's origin is its placement in the second quarter of the nineteenth century. Those decades resonate as the period of Jacksonian Democracy, the era of Manifest Destiny, America's Second Great Awakening, and America's First Industrial Revolution. Also significant, while perhaps unforeseeable at the time, baseball's foundation was laid just a generation before the United States was pitched into Civil War.

Jacksonian Democracy arose with the election of Andrew Jackson to the presidency – the beginning of American government by the people rather than American government for the people as Jackson employed notions of fairness and equality to prioritize issues and rights of the common man above those of American aristocracy. The public's participation in government was expanded as the nation expanded geographically as well. As nationalism rose, so did the importance of the role of the average American. Working-class men became known as the strength of the county – they and their individualism were what was great about America – and their pastime was important too. While baseball was a game that finally took shape in the cities, its field and equipment connected to its history of yeomen farmers. The fact that any player, playing any position, no matter their size, shape or power, could not only participate, but also be the hero of the game, paralleled the greatness of baseball to the greatness of America which thrived upon the participation of its citizens. America's Second Great Awakening, also taking place during the 1830s and 1840s, called for American Christians to become more engaged in the civic issues of their times while new sects rose to meet the needs and perspective of the population. At the same time, baseball offered a competitive release from social causes and conflicting ideologies – a common ground for a population facing increasing divisions. As the population crept westward, baseball was a factor that could move with the people and continue to unite the population. The growth of the game, like the growth of the country, had no end in sight. The first industrial revolution, with its focus upon textiles, railroads, iron and coal drew men together for labor, allowing them to indulge in team athletics, and the Manifest Destiny that followed declared the expansion of the United States and Americanism, of which baseball had become a part, to be both justifiable and inevitable.

Baseball had become intertwined with Americanism during this period because the game reflected the ideology of the men who played it. Thus, according to Horace Traubel, in 1888 Walt Whitman, one of America's most important and influential poets, said to him, "I like your interest in sports—ball, chiefest of all—baseball particularly: baseball is our game: the American game: I connect it with our national character." The equality realized by the players, as an out could be recorded by any fielder and the lineup turned over in a manner that could place any batter in the position to be a hero, compared favorably to the practices of democracy and civic responsibility where all votes counted and all men could be called upon to contribute to the nation's success. The lack of artificial time limits allowed the game to progress organically, and its season, beginning in the spring and drawing to the close in the fall, paralleled the agricultural cycle that most Americans lived by, and indeed the cycle of life in general. A game where a great batsman would still fail in the majority of his chances spoke to the determination of a young nation and the men within it as they continually faced challenge from within the county, outside the country, and from nature and the land itself. Furthermore, the importance of individualism to American nationhood was directly reflected in the great team sport where the ability to triumph would so often rest in the hands of individual batsmen. Baseball and the United States had grown with each other and in each other's likeness, though neither was yet in final form.

Indeed, while the rules of baseball were standardized and distinguished from those of other bat and ball games during the 1830s and 1840s, and a wide range of variations existed from one community to the next, they are rules that would be bizarre to today's players, though the game itself would be recognizable. Until the 1880s, batters could request either a high or a low pitch, and the pitcher was obligated to oblige while pitching underhand. At about the time those rules were changed, bats were allowed to have one flat surface, providing hitters with what today would be seen as another significant advantage. On the other hand, balls caught after the first bounce, even if they were foul, were considered fly-outs – an approach that would significantly lower the batting averages of generations that followed. Originally a game would last until one team scored twenty-one runs, a concept that would invoke nightmares among modern pace-of-game critics, the nine-inning limitation not arising until 1857. To monitor the game, there was a single umpire, seated comfortably a short distance away from home place, generally finely dressed, upstanding members of the local community. Umpires would not call balls and strikes until 1858, initially leaving the decision to swing to the batter, and they were accorded the best food and beer available at the game, as well as the clear respect of all players involved.

Still, baseball was baseball. In most forms, three strikes meant an out and three outs meant the end of the half-inning. The infield took the shape of a diamond, comprised by three bases and home plate. By 1857, the game had been standardized in New York with nine innings, nine players for each team, and ninety feet between bases – the perfect distance to preserve the exciting dispute of base hits even under 21st century replay conditions.

And then came the American Civil War, a painful but necessary episode both to maintain the Union and to popularize baseball as America's national game. Of course, the game was already firmly established in American life before shots were fired at Fort Sumner, and during the course of the War, established baseball teams were not able to maintain their regular schedule of games. However, the game was played in both Union and Confederate camps, as it had been played in the Mexican War, and as earlier bat and ball games had been played at Valley Forge. Though many more accounts of games exist from Union soldiers, it is clear that men on both sides indulged in the game, which served as a respite from the War and provided a taste of home. Baseball weeklies were published to extend baseball's influence on leisure even further, and comparisons of talents and teams were made over a significantly broader geographic area than they had been previously. Played mostly in winter camps as spring came on, baseball experienced an incredibly significant stage in its development during the War: its rules were standardized. The 'New York Rules' came to govern the game that had previously known tremendous variation in countless communities throughout the nation.

The decades that followed the Civil War were those of urbanization and the Second Industrial Revolution, and as a result, they further transitioned the game of the American people into a national pastime. The country flocked to baseball as part of a return to normalcy after Appomattox. 1866 was a year of record attendance, and each year into the next decade, attendance continued to climb. By the end of the 1860s, Cincinnati had demonstrated the possibilities of organizing professional teams, and by the 1870s, the game truly became a business. Railroads allowed communities to travel to challenge one another, and the telegraph allowed results to be relayed with efficiency. Baseball was booming with no end in sight. As Harold Seymour wrote, noting the growth of the baseball sporting goods industry in the late 19th century, "After the Civil War, bats and balls were purchased by the hundreds and thousands, whereas before they were bought by the dozen or singly." As people moved to cities, baseball offered a vestige of pastoral life. For the factory workers, it was an available escape from their new reality of challenging hours and wages. For men of varying backgrounds and origins, the diamond offered a venue for competition where talent and hustle built success. Children played the game in lots and school yards, gamblers found that there were bets to be made and money to be had, and even the newly maturing field of advertising found that baseball had much to offer it. By the late 19th century, baseball was secure as part of the American lifestyle throughout the country.

This book is about the next element developed in baseball's evolution: the development of superstar players. For, while the game is accessible to all, some players excel to such an extent that they eventually become immortals of the game. The eighteen players profiled in this book entered the game in the late nineteenth century and left it before Babe Ruth, the sport's biggest icon, entered professional baseball in 1914. They pre-date the golden era of Ruth, Cobb, Mathewson and Wagner, but standardization of rules, new transportation infrastructure, an urbanized fan base, and many other aspects combined to provide these men an opportunity to play baseball under circumstances that brought them the game's earliest nation-wide fame and notoriety. In return, their talents and ingenuity propelled the game into the modern era. They navigated the development of professional leagues and set standards for excellence that allow many of them to still be included in conversations of baseball greatness. Today, each of them has a plaque in the National Baseball Hall of Fame in Cooperstown, but those plaques are only able to convey the highlights of their great careers. In an effort to revive the essence of who they were and how they approached the game, in an effort to provide context to their immortality, these are their stories.

ADRIAN CONSTANTINE "CAP" ANSON

Cap Anson was arguably an inherent pioneer, and man destined to act as a forerunner for generations to follow. After all, in April 1851, his father, Henry, founded the town of Marshalltown, proclaiming the site to be the "the prettiest place in Iowa," which at that point had been a state for only five years. It was in a log cabin in Marshalltown that Adrian was born on April 17, 1852, the eldest Anson child and the first child born in the town. He was named Adrian Constantine after two of his father's favorite towns in southern Michigan. Half a century later, he would be known throughout the United States simply as Cap.

Adrian was a strong red-haired boy who did not enjoy school or his chores. Sadly, his mother died when he was seven years old, leaving Henry Anson alone to raise Adrian and his brother Sturgis. During those years, the Civil War raged in the United States, and Iowa, a free state, sided with the North. At the same time, while many Iowans were abolitionists, they were concerned about the effects of abolition, believing that whites were a superior race and not wanting other races to live alongside them. Instead, in those early years, they wanted slavery abolished so that African-Americans could be removed from American society, thereby creating a very distinct racial separation in the society that Adrian knew in his youth. During that time, in the Anson household, the boys had grown to become trouble-makers, and, hoping to curb their wildness, their father sent them to a high school aged boarding school at the University of Notre Dame in 1865, when Adrian was fourteen years old. During breaks from school, Adrian played baseball, a relatively new sport, and he managed to earn a spot on his hometown team, the Marshalltown Stars, at the age of 15. Adrian was enrolled at Notre Dame for two years, but he did not do well in school as he preferred baseball and other sports over studying. In 1867, he left Notre Dame and returned home to Marshalltown.

1868 provided a landmark moment in Adrian's life as he and the Marshalltown Stars won the Iowa State Championship. Adrian played second base on the team, and it was truly a family affair as his father played third base and his brother, Sturgis, was the center fielder. Still, his father did not believe that baseball offered a future for his son, and Adrian was sent to the University of Iowa. However, Adrian was asked to leave the university after only one semester because of poor behavior. Once again he returned to Marshalltown, where he probably worked for one of his father's businesses and, of course, played baseball. It was a time of great change. Following the Civil War, Iowa allowed all races to vote before being required to by Constitutional Amendment when, in 1868, Iowans approved an amendment removing the word "white" as a requirement for voting in Iowa. That same year, black children were allowed to attend public schools following a lawsuit by the Clark family of Muscatine, Iowa. However, it would not be until 1884 that the Iowa legislature passed a law that declared theatres, hotels, restaurants and other public services should not discriminate against blacks or any other race. In the midst of all of that change, Adrian must have felt a great deal of uncertainty regarding his own life. In 1870, it was baseball that opened the door to his future fame, although he surely did not recognize it at the time. However, even within the confines of professional baseball, Anson would eventually find himself in conflict with the nation's new racial realities.

Rockford Illinois' team, the Forest Citys, had become one of the great baseball teams of the American Midwest. Led by their star right-handed pitcher Al Spalding, they had won a number of important tournaments and even defeated the National Champion Cincinnati Red Stocking. In pursuit of more success, the Forest Citys came to Marshalltown in the summer of 1870 with plans to dominate the Iowa state champions. The Marshalltown Stars were seriously over-matched and, in front of a tremendous crowd, some of whom had traveled all the way from Chicago, they lost the game 18-3. Nevertheless, the game was a significant achievement for the Stars as the superior Forest Citys had been expected to win by 30 to 50 runs. As a result, while their team had won the game, many Rockford fans had lost money after betting on the game's final score. In order to allow those fans an opportunity to win their money back, a second game was arranged and played on the following day. Again Marshalltown lost, this time 35-5, but Rockford had had an opportunity to watch the Marshalltown talent over the course of two games, and they were impressed by what they had seen, especially by the Ansons. In fact, when reflecting on those two games many years later, Al Spalding said, "We found that the main strength of the Marshalltown team was the Anson family… they put up a rattling game, especially the two sons, and they were the hardest fighters I ever saw in my life." It was at this point that Adrian apparently realized that he may be able to make a living playing the game that he loved. After receiving his father's blessing to play baseball for money, if he could do so honestly, Adrian began to write to professional teams to request a try-out. None, however, were interested in such a young player with no professional experience.

Once again, Adrian was granted opportunity by Rockford's Forest Citys, who had decided to become part of a professional league. At the same time, several of its best players, including Al Spalding, were recruited to other teams that could offer them more money. As a result, the Forest Citys were in need of strong players, and they well-remembered the strength and toughness of the Anson family, so they offered all three Ansons, Henry and his two sons, professional baseball contracts. While the Ansons must have been flattered, only Adrian accepted the offer. His father, at 44, thought it more prudent to stay in Marshalltown and attend to his business interests, and brother Sturgis had previously hurt his arm and seemed to know that he would likely not be able to achieve stardom. Adrian, however, had his chance at last. Following a winter of practice in his father's barn, in 1871, with the nickname "The Marshalltown Infant", Adrian joined the Rockford Forest Citys at age 19 as a professional baseball player. He played third base and batted .325, but the Forest Citys finished the season in last place, and the team was disbanded.

Still, Adrian's career was far from over, and he was quickly signed by the Philadelphia Athletics to join them for the 1872 season. At more than six feet high and weighing 200 pounds or more, Adrian was generally considered to be the biggest and strongest player of the decade, and in 1872 he began to achieve national fame as he posted a batting average of .415, which was to be the highest of his career. In addition to finding professional achievement in Philadelphia over the next four seasons, Adrian would find love as well, as he began a relationship with Virginia Fiegal, the teenage daughter of a saloon owner. In the midst of his success, Adrian and the Philadelphia A's were invited to travel to England with the Boston Red Stockings in 1874. Harry Wright, the Red Stockings' manager and center fielder, had come to America from England, and it was his dream to take the game that he loved back to the land of his birth. Thus, as they traveled, both teams played exhibitions of baseball and cricket. Again, Anson distinguished himself as he led both teams in batting average during the tour. In addition, he was also able to build a deeper friendship with Al Spalding, who at that time was pitching for the Red Stockings. The following season was to be Adrian's final season in Philadelphia, but it was an important one. After having played so well and having become a leader of the Athletics on the field, Adrian spent the 1875 season as the Athletics' manager as well as their star player. He led his team to a second-place finish in the National Association with 53 wins and only 20 losses. However, despite the team's great play, Adrian had to face change once again as the National Association folded. The Philadelphia Athletics would eventually join the newly formed National League the next year, but during the period of uncertainty and transition, Adrian had received an offer he could not refuse and returned to his native Midwest to play baseball in Chicago.

Cap Anson, 1887
Allen & Ginter World's Champions (N28)
Courtesy of Library of Congress PPOC

Al Spalding had signed with the Chicago White Stockings in 1875, and he served as their manager in 1876. It was Spalding who recommended Anson to team ownership, and they signed him to a contract while his future in Philadelphia seemed uncertain. Unbeknownst to them, Anson would remain with the Chicago team for the remainder of his playing career. Under Spalding's management, Anson batted .325 and was part of a pennant winning White Stockings team in 1876 with a 52-14 record, but it was a challenging time for him personally. Virginia Fiegal, with whom he had fallen in love, was upset with him for moving away, so much so that Anson attempted to be released from his White Stockings contract, even offering to pay $1000 for his release. Chicago, however, would not relinquish him, as he was one of their star players, and Adrian's relationship with Virginia was in jeopardy. Ultimately, rather than lose Virginia, Adrian asked her to marry him, and the two were wed on November 21. The marriage lasted almost forty years, until Virginia's death in 1915, with the couple initially living in Chicago during the baseball season and Philadelphia in the off-season, until they moved to Chicago full time in the mid-1880s.

In all, Anson would go on to play 22 seasons for the White Stockings team, who became the Chicago Cubs in 1903 after having also been known as Anson's Colts (1890-1897) and the Chicago Remnants or Orphans (1898-1902) upon Anson's retirement. That Chicago team is the only franchise to have remained in the same city since the formation of the National League in 1876.

Cap Anson, 1887
Allen & Ginter World's Champions (N28)
Courtesy of Library of Congress PPOC

11

With Chicago, Anson would go on to capture four batting titles, also finishing second for the honor in several other seasons, and he led the league in runs batted in eight times. He was clearly the best player manning first base on one of baseball's best teams, and his tenure with the club helped to build him into a strong and recognizable sports figure on the national level. In all, he had sixteen season ranking in the top ten players for hits, twenty seasons in the top ten in batting average, fifteen seasons in the top ten for doubles, seven seasons in the top ten for homeruns, and sixteen seasons in the top ten for runs batted in. Anson also managed the Chicago team for 19 seasons, fully making the transition from Adrian to Cap (a shorted version of Captain used early in his managerial career) to Pop as he mentored his young players, including such superstars as Mike Kelly.

Anson became the first major-league player credited with 3,000 hits, though there is some dispute about his actual career total, which varies somewhat from source to source because of dubious record-keeping of the period, dispute over whether to count 5 hits that Anson obtained while playing in the National Association (for the Rockford Forest Citys), and because of a rule that existed only in 1887 wherein walks were counted as hits.

Unfortunately, in addition to all of the talent that he brought to the game of baseball, Anson also brought the prejudices of his youth. He is credited, through his celebrity and influence, with helping to introduce a policy of racial segregation that infected baseball until Jackie Robinson joined the Brooklyn Dodgers more than sixty years later. Anson's involvement in baseball's segregation began with an August 1883 game that his Chicago White Stockings played against the minor league Toledo Blue Stockings. While more than fifty African-Americans are recorded as playing professional baseball at the time, the Toledo team featured a strong-fielding catcher named Moses "Fleetwood" Walker who was one of the first African-Americans in the major leagues. Anson flatly refused to share the playing field with an African-American player. In order for the game to continue, Toledo did not allow Walker to play, and that situation was repeated when Anson's teams played against Walker in subsequent years. Despite the fact that Walker and his younger brother made it to the Major Leagues in 1884, when Toledo joined the American Association, other star players soon began taking the position that Cap Anson had taken and refused to play against them. The Walkers were out of baseball by 1889, and baseball's age of segregation had begun through unwritten agreement, in part by the race protest of Adrian "Cap" Anson.

Adrian C. Anson, *America's National Game*, pg. 178

It is also known that, during his time as a player and manager, Anson placed bets on baseball with many of those bets placed on his own team, a practice that would not be tolerated by later generations. However, they were relatively commonplace and accepted at the time, as long as one did not bet against his own team or accept a bribe to play poorly or to purposely lose a game. For example, star pitcher Jim Devlin was banned from professional baseball for life after being found to have thrown games for money as a member of the 1877 Louisville Grays. It was not until 1927, in the months following an alleged cheating scandal featuring greats Ty Cobb and Tris Speaker, that Commissioner Kennesaw Mountain Landis proposed rules against gambling in baseball, including "permanent ineligibility for betting any sum whatsoever upon any ball game in connection with which the bettor has any duty to perform." In his time, Anson faced no such rule. Thus, while he is now recognized as the player/manager who, by far, placed the most bets on baseball games during the 1880s and 1890s, there have never been allegations that Cap Anson accepted a bribe or participated in the fixing of any games. On the contrary, his legacy is one that involves him as having perhaps the greatest integrity of his era.

During the 1891 season, Cap may actually have been the victim of collusion that cost his team the pennant. Anson's devotion to the Chicago National League team had not been impacted by major league baseball players' attempt to unionize in the late 1880s, and he had not joined the union's Players' League for the 1890 season. 1891 was a dominant season for Anson's Colts, who finished with a record of 82-53 (Anson himself had led the league in runs batted in), but they fell to a second-place finish as the Boston Beaneaters finished at 87-51. Much was made of a late-season series with the New York Giants that had contributed to Boston's success, as New York committed 25 errors and surrendered 51 runs in the first four games of a five-game series while not playing many of their best players. Anson and other members of the Chicago team protested in vain as news organizations such as the *Cincinnati Post* posited, "New York played winning ball until it saw that Chicago would win the pennant." Anson's anti-union stance and the low pay for Chicago players had apparently served as motivators. As a result, the Chicago pennant earned in 1876, Anson's first year with the club, and the five that he won as a player-manager from 1880 to 1886 would be Anson's only National League first-place finishes.

Following his baseball career, Cap worked in vaudeville and attempted several different business ventures in the Chicago area, but they were largely not successful. On the other hand, in 1904 he captained a team that won the American Bowling Congress National Title, which made him the only man to win national championships in more than one professional sport. He also entered politics, championing Republicans like William McKinley and Theodore Roosevelt at the national level while associating with the Democratic Party at the local level, through which he was elected as Chicago city clerk. Nonetheless, his business failures continued. Despite financial need, during which he filed two bankruptcies and lost his home, he refused offers of pensions from Major League Baseball and assistance from friends because he felt they would tarnish his manhood. In June 1907, at age 55, in an attempt to boost attendance and revenue, he even returned to the playing field as the first baseman for Anson's Colts, a Chicago City League team that he owned, but that effort was not enough. So, instead, he continued acting in vaudeville until his full retirement in 1921. He died on April 14, 1922, just three days short of his seventieth birthday, in St. Luke's hospital following an operation for a glandular condition. He is buried in Oak Woods Cemetery in Chicago. He was remembered by his long-time friend Al Spalding as "one of the greatest ball players that ever lived – and a man whose word was always as good as his bond."

Almost one hundred years after his death, Cap is still the Chicago Cubs' all-time leader for average (.339), hits (3,081), singles (2,330), doubles (530), runs (1,712), and RBI (1,879).

1876 Chicago White Stockings

1888 Chicago White Stockings

Professional Debut: May 06, 1871, for the Rockford Forest Citys

Final Major League Game: October 03, 1897, for the Chicago Cubs

Career Batting Average: .334

4-time NL Batting Champion: .317 in 1879, .381 in 1881, .347 in 1887 and .344 in 1888

Career Hits: somewhere in the range of 2,995-3,435; MLB credits him with 3,081

Career Homeruns: 97

Career RBI: 2,075; 8-time NL RBI Leader: 1880-82, 1884-86, 1888, and 1891

Inducted to the Major League Baseball Hall of Fame: 1939

Anson's Hall of Fame Plaque Reads:

ADRIAN CONSTANTINE ANSON
"CAP"
GREATEST HITTER AND GREATEST
NATIONAL LEAGUE PLAYER-MANAGER
OF 19TH CENTURY. STARTED WITH
CHICAGOS IN NATIONAL LEAGUE'S
FIRST YEAR 1876. CHICAGO MANAGER
FROM 1879 TO 1897, WINNING 5 PENNANTS.
WAS .300 CLASS HITTER 20 YEARS,
BATTING CHAMPION 4 TIMES.

JACOB PETER "JAKE" BECKLEY

Hannibal, Missouri, is perhaps best known for its connection to Samuel Clemens, the writer who would eventually be known world-wide as Mark Twain. After all, Twain spent his formative years, from age four to eighteen, in Hannibal, and the town inspired the settings for some of his most notable fiction, including *Tom Sawyer and Huckleberry Finn*. Less well-known is the fact that Hannibal was also the hometown of Hall of Famer Jake Beckley, one of baseball's greatest hitters of the late-19th and early-20th centuries. For twenty years, Beckley would set records and leave his mark on the major leagues, and while he passed at the early age of fifty, he led a life that allowed him to witness America's transition from simple village life to the wielder of world power in the midst of the Great War.

Born on August 4, 1867, Beckley was just nine years old when *Tom Sawyer* was published, an age easily associating him with the children of Twain's tale. One could easily imagine him turning out his pockets for treasure that he could trade for a turn at the grand task of whitewashing a picket fence. However, any such pursuits would not captivate Beckley for long, as he quickly took to the game of baseball, beginning his play with semi-professional teams while still a teenager. He was first suggested by Bob Hart, a former Hannibal teammate, to the Leavenworth Oilers of Kansas. Thus, at eighteen, like Samuel Clemens several years before, Beckley left Hannibal to pursue his profession. The city that had been the first of territorial Kansas, later the center of America's slavery dispute and the supply base that helped to open the American West, became the first of what would be many homes in Beckley's baseball career.

Naturally left-handed and stocky in build (he played much of his career at 5'10", 200 lbs.), Beckley was surprisingly quick. His one notable limitation was a weak throwing arm, which soon limited his positioning in the field to first base, and his greatest asset was undoubtedly his bat. During

1887, Beckley's second season, which he split between Leavenworth and another Western League team in Lincoln Nebraska, walks were counted as hits, and Beckley batted above .400. That success propelled interest in Beckley, and after he had a chance to play just 34 games with the St. Louis Whites to begin 1888, he was purchased, along with a teammate, by the Pittsburgh Alleghenies, in only their second year with the National League, for the tremendous sum of $4500, and Beckley's career in the major leagues began. The twenty-year-old rookie quickly proved up to the task, batting .343 in seventy-one games. During the following season, he further proved that his rookie campaign had not been a fluke, as he again batted above .300 while playing first base for a full season, also finishing in the league's top ten for triples, homeruns, and runs batted in. Before long, Beckley was granted the nickname Eagle-Eye for his talent as a batsman.

Then, even more quickly than it began, it seemed that Jake Beckley's major league career was at an end. In 1890, Beckley left the Alleghenies to play for the newly formed Pittsburgh Burghers of the Players' League, famously explaining, "I'm only in this game for the money anyway," as he changed teams only upon the Burghers' promise of a higher salary. Beckley finished in the league's top 10 in hits, doubles, triples, homeruns, and runs batted in, while batting .323, but the Burghers finished in sixth place (of eight) with a losing record, and despite good attendance the Players' League folded after only a single season because its team owners did not have the confidence to extend their investments. As a result, it was assumed that the stars of the Players' League would return to the teams for which they had played previously, but for Beckley and other former members of the Alleghenies, that turned out to not exactly be the case. During the transition, the Alleghenies also acquired second baseman Lou Bierbauer, who had played with the American Association's Philadelphia Athletics before his stint in the Players' League. Though they had not formally resigned Bierbauer or included him on their reserve list, the Philadelphia Athletics were irate at the Alleghenies' actions, famously describing them as "piratical". The Alleghenies proudly owned their actions to such an extent that it embraced the controversy as the identifying factor for the rebuilt club, and at the age of twenty-three, Eagle-Eye Beckley found himself a member of the first Pittsburgh Pirates baseball club.

Jake Beckley, 1887-1890
Old Judge (N172)
Courtesy of Library of Congress PPOC

Not long thereafter, tragedy struck as Beckley lost his young bride, Molly, to tuberculosis just months after their 1891 marriage, doubtlessly contributing to struggles at the plate in 1892 as he batted a career low .236. Nonetheless, Eagle-Eye would average 28 doubles, 19 triples, 106 runs and 101 runs batted in for his first five seasons as a Pirate. He was a fan favorite and a true star of the National League, but those sentiments would not spare him the consequences of a slumping 1896 season which saw his batting average dip once again as his power numbers also faded. He was traded to the New York Giants for right-handed first baseman Harry Davis and $1000 cash. His numbers improved in the latter part of the season, but they dipped again in early 1897, leading the Giants to release him in May.

Fortunately for Beckley, the Cincinnati Reds were in need of a first baseman, so they signed him just weeks after his release, allowing his major league career to continue. His move to Cincinnati, where he would spend six and a half seasons, revitalized him, as his batting average and run production returned to form even as major league baseball entered the dead-ball era. Eagle-Eye's seminal moment came on September 26, 1897, as he became the first Cincinnati Red to hit three homeruns in a single game. Beckley's feat occurred in the first game of a doubleheader against the St. Louis Browns, a doubleheader that Cincinnati swept on their way to a 76-56 record for the season. Interestingly, the three-homerun game is not the element of the 1897 season that features most prominently in Jake Beckley's storied career. Instead, that designation belongs to a game that the Reds played against the Louisville Colonels who had a twenty-three-year-old rookie named Honus Wagner, who was already impacting the league on his way to a .335 average for the season.

For years, Beckley had enjoyed using a hidden ball trick, in multiple variations, against rookies whenever he had the chance. However, Honus Wagner was no typical rookie as he entered the league an elite player. When Beckley attempted to employ his trick against Wagner, the exact sequence of events is unclear – either Wagner cannily spotted the trick or Beckley reached under the wrong corner of the base, under which he had hidden the ball, and bungled the trick himself. In any event, it is clear that the trick did not work and that the rookie got the better of the renowned veteran in the moment. He rose to the challenge of Wagner's baseball intelligence, employing a double ball trick in a later meeting between the two. In that meeting, after Wagner had reached first, Beckley went to his position with a ball tucked under his arm, as though he were trying to hide it, but at the same time ensuring that the astute Wagner would see it. With the umpires' attention focused elsewhere, Wagner grabbed for the ball and threw it away. As Wagner proceeded towards second, he found himself an easy out as the Cincinnati pitcher had held the true game ball the entire time.

The Wagner incidents are not unique in illustrating the character that Beckley brought to the ballfield. Surprisingly quick considering his stocky body, Beckley stole 315 bases during his major league career. On occasion, he would also advantage his team by cutting across the infield while running the bases if the umpires did not keep a diligent watch. Beckley's most notable employment of this trick happened in a game umpired by Tim Hurst, a combative, long-tenured umpire who had also managed the St. Louis Browns during the 1898 season. While Hurst's attention was directed elsewhere, Beckley cut across the infield from second base to home, sliding across the plate without a play being made on him. Hurst called him out anyway, purportedly shouting, "You big son of a bitch, you got here too fast!"

Jake Beckley, 1887-1890
Old Judge (N172)
Courtesy of Library of Congress PPOC

    Still, Beckley's quickness and hustle were a serious part of his game, sometimes necessary to compensate for less flattering attributes, such as his poor throwing arm. Following his time with the Cincinnati Reds, Beckley played first base for the St. Louis Cardinals to conclude his major league career. During that time, in a game against the Pittsburgh Pirates, speedster Tommy Leach dropped a bunt down the first base line that Beckley was forced to field. Beckley then spun and threw the ball far out of the reach of Jack Taylor, the pitcher who was covering first. At that point, Leach blazed around the bases in an attempt to score (49 of his 63 career homeruns were inside-the-park), and Beckley raced to pursue the ball in foul territory. Upon retrieving it, rather than risking another throw, Beckley raced to meet Leach at the plate. When the dust cleared, Leach was out, and he had two broken ribs for his trouble.

    Eagle-Eye Beckley was himself an accomplished bunter. He even developed a unique method of flipping his bat while a pitch was being delivered to home plate so that he could bunt the ball with the bat's handle while holding it by the barrel, a technique requiring both skill and fearlessness. Beckley's fearlessness was tested directly in a July 8, 1901, game against the New York Giants and their young hurler, Christy Mathewson. While Mathewson is now regarded as one of the best pitchers that the game has ever known, in part, due to his excellent fastball and outstanding control, in 1901 he was in the midst of his first full season, a season that would see him hit thirteen batters, a career high, while also leading the league with twenty-three wild pitches. On that Monday afternoon, as the New York Giants were on their way to defeating the Reds in an effort to avoid last-place standing, a Mathewson fastball struck Beckley in the head, leaving him unconscious for more than five minutes. Eagle-Eye's future was immediately in question, but he missed only two games because of the injury, and he finished the season with an average of .307 before continuing on with an average of .327 over the next three seasons.

Beckley left the Cincinnati Reds following the 1903 season as Reds manager Joe Kelley sought playing time for himself at first base. During his eight years with the team, Eagle-Eye batted .325 with 77 triples, 592 runs scored, and 570 runs batted in. Despite his poor throwing arm, or perhaps because of it, he also had one appearance as a starting pitcher on the final day of the 1902 season. On that day, in poor weather, the Pittsburgh Pirates would finish the season with a 27.5 game lead over the second-place Brooklyn Superbas, having secured the pennant weeks before. The Cincinnati Reds, on the other hand, were finishing a season of .500 ball, and they had no desire to play the final game in rainy, muddy conditions. When the Pirates refused to cancel the game, the Reds played their players out of their regular positions, thereby landing Beckley his stint on the pitcher's mound. He would carry the loss, giving up eight runs (only three earned) on nine hits over four innings while striking out two and walking one. From then on, it would be first base, and only first base, for Beckley.

At first, Beckley's play for the St. Louis Cardinals was effective, as his 1904 numbers were consistent with those he had produced in the few seasons prior. However, age did eventually catch up with Eagle-Eye, and as he approached the age of forty, he found that his role on the team, and his overall effectiveness, were decreasing. He played his final major league game on June 15, 1907, and he retired with more games played at first base than any other player, a record that would stand until 1994, the career lead for triples, a category in which he still ranks as fourth, and ranking second in hits only to the great Cap Anson.

Having played baseball for his entire adult life, stepping away from the game was not easy for Beckley. For years, he moved around Kansas and Missouri playing on minor league and independent teams (winning the

American Association batting title in 1907), managing, coaching and umpiring. It was not until 1914 that he stepped away from the game, moving to Kansas City to operate a grain business. He married, but the couple did not have any children. When a Cincinnati company had suspicions about their middle-age customer with no apparent background in business and inquired as to why his name could not be found in Dun and Bradstreet, a company who published objective, centralized credit reports, Beckley replied, "Look in the Spalding Baseball Guide for any of the last twenty years." Indeed, during his two decades in the National League, Beckley had established himself as one of the game's greats.

Jake Eagle-Eye Beckley died of heart disease in Kansas City on June 25, 1918. His body was interred in his hometown of Hannibal, Missouri, bringing Beckley back to the town of his birth. However, the world had changed during the course of his life. The second industrial revolution and competing imperialist interests had culminated in the Great War. Just three weeks after his passing, the Second Battle of the Marne, the last major German offensive on the Western Front, would begin. The novels of Mark Twain that had captivated readers with tales exploring the American identity had given way to poetry and novels used to convey the sufferings and horrors of war. Like the town of Hannibal, Jake Beckley was no longer in the spotlight of American interest despite his contributions and his importance. More than another fifty years would pass until Beckley was inducted into the Baseball Hall of Fame by the Veterans Committee in 1971.

Professional Debut: June 20, 1888, for the Pittsburgh Alleghenys

Final Major League Game: June 15, 1907, for the St. Louis Cardinals

Career Batting Average: .309

Career Hits: 2,930

Career Triples: 244

Career RBI: 1,578

Inducted to the Major League Baseball Hall of Fame: 1971

Beckley's Hall of Fame Plaque Reads:

JACOB PETER BECKLEY
"OLD EAGLE EYE"
1888-1907
FAMED NATIONAL LEAGUE SLUGGER
MADE 2,930 HITS FOR LIFETIME .309 BATTING
AVERAGE. HOLDS RECORD IN MAJORS FOR
FIRST BASE: FOR CHANCES ACCEPTED 25,000,
MOST PUTOUTS 23,696, MOST GAMES 2,368
PLAYED 20 SEASONS WITH PITTSBURGH,
NEW YORK, CINCINNATI, AND ST. LOUIS.

DENNIS JOSEPH "DAN" BROUTHERS

Francis Richter founded the weekly magazine *Sporting Life* in 1883 to provide coverage of various sports with a specific emphasis on baseball. In 1914, Richter published a book entitled *History and Records of Baseball: the American Nation's Chief Sport*. In that book, Richter provided his rankings of the greatest baseball players of each decade by position. For first basemen of the decade 1890-1900, Richter named two players as being superior to all others: Jake Beckley and Dan Brouthers. However, the pathways that the two men took to their success differed greatly. While Beckley's rise to major league success was rapid and seemingly assured, Brouthers met an early disaster that almost derailed his professional baseball career.

Dan Brouthers was born on May 8, 1858, in Sylvan Lake, New York, a hamlet named for the Ice Age lake upon whose shores it was built. He is said to have played baseball from an early age in games organized in Sylvan Lake's sandlots. Brouthers was very powerful, weighing in at slightly over 200 pounds on his 6'2" frame, and that size and power allowed him to develop as a slugger in a time when the game baseball was premised on contact and speed. Known for the driving power of his shoulders and his skill with the bat, Brouthers began to play semi-professionally, as both a pitcher and first baseman, as a teenager in Wappingers Falls, New York. It was in the fifth inning of a July 7, 1877, game in Wappingers Falls against the Harlem Clippers that Brouthers' time in the game almost ended, hardly having yet begun.

Brouthers, who was on third base, broke for home when his teammate put the ball into play, only to find home plate blocked by Clippers' catcher Johnny Quigley. The two collided, and Quigley was terribly injured as the left side of his forehead was struck by Brouthers' knee. Quigley fell, was helped to his feet, and then went to the ground again while bleeding profusely. Quigley was quickly carried to the home of local physician Dr.

James M. Cosgrove, who had been in attendance at the game. Another physician was called in to assist, and it was determined that Quigley's fontal bone had been severely damaged and knocked in, which the doctors diagnosed to be fatal. Quigley's mother was sent for, which led to the realization that she was a widow living with young children in a very poor Harlem neighborhood. The young catcher was the family's only wage earner. Determined to save Quigley's life, the doctors operated and removed several fragments of his skull. Throughout all of this, Dan Brouthers was a nearly constant visitor to Quigley, who remained conscious, and following the surgery, Quigley's state began to improve, even to the point where he began to talk about playing baseball again. However, an infection eventually set in, and Quigley's injuries ultimately overwhelmed him. He died on August 12, more than a month after the collision. On the following day, Brouthers faced a formal inquiry about the accident, but he was absolved of all guilt. The Wappingers Falls Actives paid the cost of Quigley's coffin and to transport his body back to Harlem where a fundraiser baseball game between Harlem teams raised money for his family. Still, Brouthers was devastated, and he quit baseball two months before the 1877 season ended, intending to never play again.

It is unclear what changed Brouthers' mind about baseball, but he did rejoin his Wappingers Falls team in 1878. What is clear is that he never escaped the tragedy of Johnny Quigley's death. The memory haunted him for the remainder of his life, and on several occasions, as he rose to fame, he would have to relive it as it would be rekindled by the press. Despite his return, Brouthers would not finish the 1878 season with Wappingers Falls, as the memory of Johnny Quigley's death haunted him with every home game he played. By August, he accepted an offer to move across the state and to play for a team in Scottsville, NY, where his first known homerun was recorded on August 24.

Brouthers made his major league debut for the Troy Trojans on June 23, 1879. In 39 games, he batted .274, also hitting twelve doubles and four homeruns (the league leader hit nine in eighty-three games). The twenty-one-year-old primarily played first base, though he struggled with thirty-three errors in thirty-seven games. He also pitched in three games, but he gave up thirty runs (thirteen were earned) in twenty-one innings while striking out only six. Despite his struggles in the field and on the mound, because of his offensive success, it was a surprise when Brouthers was released from the team during the season's final week, a decision possibly explained by his struggles to adjust to a new Troy manager. His release from Troy meant a return to the minors for most of the 1880 season. Brouthers hit well enough to earn a second chance with the Trojans, but his second chance ended with his second release when he managed just two singles in twelve at-bats.

Nonetheless, Brouthers remained in the major leagues for the 1881 season, his breakout year, though he played in only 65 games. He signed with the Buffalo Bisons, and he batted .319 while leading the league in homeruns (8, despite having only 270 at-bats) and slugging (.541). More importantly, Brouthers found a baseball home where he could establish his career. He spent five seasons with Buffalo, leading the league in slugging each of those years. He won batting titles and, in 1883, he broke Cap Anson's single season record for RBI. Playing first base, he was one of the Big Four, perhaps the strongest group of teammates in the era, along with Jack Rowe (catcher), Hardy Richardson (second base), and Deacon White (third base). However, even the force of the Big Four couldn't deliver a pennant to Buffalo, and the team began to experience financial difficulties which led to the selling off of players. The Big Four remained a powerful unit, selling collectively to the Detroit Wolverines of the National League for a total of $7000.

"Dan" Brouthers, *America's National Game*, pg. 278

In Detroit, the Big Four continued their dominance, and for his part, Brouthers led the league in slugging, doubles, homeruns, and total bases. However, despite their offensive dominance and a record that was more than fifty games above .500, the Wolverines failed to capture a pennant. They set their eyes upon a first-place finish for 1887, but in the offseason that lay between, Brouthers found yet another way to impact baseball in a new role, one that was perhaps his most important in regard to the development of the game.

1886 had been a turbulent year for the U.S. labor movement. To begin the decade, the Knights of Labor (short for The Noble and Holy Order of the Knights of Labor) was the largest and most important American labor organization. The Knights had been formed in 1869 and welcomed members without regard to race, religion or gender in an effort to unite all workers behind common causes, prohibiting members of only five occupational groups: lawyers, bankers, land speculators, liquor dealers and gamblers. While opposing anarchism and socialism, they advocated for the 8-hour work day, against child labor, and for improved working conditions. While their leader, Terrance Powderly, initially discouraged strikes as a tactic, the Knights eventually utilized boycotts and strikes in their methods, giving a significant amount of autonomy to their local branches. Significant success in a strike against the Wabash Railroad helped the Knights' membership rise to almost 800,000 in 1886 before disaster struck. On May 4, a peaceful labor rally at Haymarket Square in Chicago devolved into chaos as an anarchist hurled a dynamite bomb at attending police, eventually leading to the deaths of seven police officers and four civilians. The bombing, when compounded with the failed Great Southwest Railroad Strike and increasing acceptance of segregationist leanings in the American south and against Chinese labor, led to the rapid decline of the Knights of Labor. They were no longer America's leading labor organization, promptly being displaced by the American Federation of Labor, an alliance of craft unions, which formed in December of 1886.

In the midst of this American labor turmoil, American baseball players also began to organize. The Brotherhood of Professional Base-Ball Players, baseball's first labor organization, had been formed in 1885 in order to support the rise of players' salaries given the game's growing success. On November 11, 1886, Brouthers was elected vice-president of the Brotherhood, serving with elected president John Montgomery Ward. The Brotherhood's goal was to gain as members as many prominent National League players as possible, and then to meet with National League ownership in order to challenge the reserve system, which restricted players' abilities to move from one team to another, and thereby kept salaries low.

Dan Brouthers, 1888
Goodwin Champions (N162)
Courtesy of Library of Congress PPOC

While working in the Brotherhood, Brouthers and the other members of the Big Four found team success, leading the Detroit Wolverines to a first-place finish before competing with the St. Louis Browns in a best-of-fifteen "World Series". Detroit won the championship, winning eight of the first eleven games, and then they completed the series, winning ten of fifteen overall. Despite his dominant numbers during the season, Brouthers was able to play only a single game in the series, securing two singles in three at-bats, but he was a champion.

Unfortunately, the success of 1886 couldn't be repeated. On November 17, the Brotherhood achieved their desired meeting with National League ownership, a meeting in which Brouthers was one of only three players involved. Negotiations were unsuccessful as owners would not make desired concessions, and the failure of the Brotherhood transformed into the Players' League by 1890, a fracturing of baseball that placed a players-owned league in direct competition with the National League for a single tumultuous season, as the American Association continued to build itself as a third alternative for professional baseball. Brouthers' success on the baseball diamond also declined. His personal offensive numbers were down in 1888, and the Wolverines finished in fifth place, and at season's end, Brouthers was purchased by the Boston Beaneaters, ending his association with the Wolverines and the Big Four.

With the transition to the Beaneaters came a return to form. Brouthers led the league in batting while striking out only six times in contrast with earning sixty-six bases on balls. He scored 105 runs and drove in 118. However, at season's end, the draw of the Brotherhood's cause outweighed the success Brouthers had found with the Boston National League team, and he left for the Boston Reds, a newly formed team of the Players' League. Featuring a very strong roster, the Boston Reds finished in first place, with Brouthers once again finishing amongst the league leaders in several offensive categories. But, regardless of the Reds' fortunes, the Players' League was done after a single season despite good attendance numbers as investors were not optimistic that it would be able to compete long-term with the National League and the American Association. Most Players' League teams were dissolved, but the Boston Reds, along with the Philadelphia Athletics, moved into the American Association, only to dissolve a year later as the American Association also failed. By 1892, at the same time that Carnegie Steel's partnership with Pinkerton Detectives and Pennsylvania state militia defeated the Homestead Strike and damaged unionization nation-wide, the National League gained more control over its players than ever through the elimination of its competition, and it would be more than a half century before professional baseball would once again be able to unionize its players. Throughout it all, Brouthers continued to perform, leading the league again in batting average and several other categories as the Boston Reds won the American Association pennant, giving him a somewhat unique distinction of winning pennants in the same city for three consecutive years while playing in three different leagues.

For the next several years, Dan Brouthers continued to produce offensively for several major league teams, though he finally faced reduced playing time in 1895 and 1896. He played with a number of future Hall of Famers, including Willie Keeler, John McGraw and Hughie Jennings, and he achieved another championship as a member of the Baltimore Orioles. Beginning in 1897, he played several more seasons in the minor leagues, completing his major league career with five at-bats over the course of two games with McGraw's New York Giants in 1904.

Dan Brouthers, 1887-1890
Old Judge (N172)
Courtesy of Library of Congress PPOC

In all, Brouthers led his league average in 1882, 1883, 1889, 1891 and 1892, leaving him even more than a century later with one of the top ten career batting averages in major league history. In 1898, Brouthers won another batting title with a .415 average for the minor league Toronto Maple Leafs. In his final season of professional ball, 1904, with Poughkeepsie, Brouthers batted .385, leading the Hudson River League. He never struck out more than thirty times in the season, more than once striking out less than ten times in seasons of more than 500 at-bats. Of course, Brouthers was not simply a contact hitter. In addition to his batting crowns, he led the major leagues in slugging seven times and was one of the top homerun hitters of his day. His offensive dominance led to him being the first major league player to be intentionally walked on a regular basis.

For more than twenty years before his death, Brouthers worked as a night watchman and manager of the press gate at the Polo Grounds, a position provided him by former Baltimore teammate John McGraw. He succumbed to a heart attack on August 2, 1932 at the age of 74. Noting that Brouthers hit over .300 for fifteen years, the *New York Times* described him in his obituary as the "Ty Cobb of his time", a former teammate of McGraw, and "one of the greatest batsmen in the history of baseball."

1894 Baltimore Orioles

Professional Debut: June 23, 1879, for the Troy Trojans

Final Major League Game: October 04, 1904, for the New York Giants

Career Batting Average: .342; led league 1882-1883, 1889, 1891-1892

Career Hits: 2,303

Career Doubles: 462; led league 1886-1888

Career Homeruns: 107; led league 1881, 1886

Career RBI: 1,301; led league 1883, 1892

Inducted to the Major League Baseball Hall of Fame: 1945

Brouthers' Hall of Fame Plaque Reads:

DAN BROUTHERS
HARD-HITTING FIRST BASEMAN OF
EIGHT MAJOR LEAGUE CLUBS, HE WAS
PART OF ORIGINAL "BIG FOUR" OF BUFFALO.
TRADED WITH OTHER MEMBERS OF
THAT COMBINATION TO DETROIT, HE HIT
.419 AS CITY WON ITS ONLY NATIONAL
LEAGUE CHAMPIONSHIP IN 1887.

JOHN GIBSON CLARKSON

A glimpse at John Clarkson's personal history suggests that he had the makings of an upper-class businessman rather than a professional athlete. Born on July 1, 1861, to a prosperous jeweler in Cambridge, Massachusetts, John could have easily accepted a place in the family business or studied at Harvard, as did at least two of his brothers. In fact, he did work at the jewelry shop following high school and attended classes at the nearby Comer's Business School. His physique also failed to suggest athletic prowess as, at his peak, he stood at five feet ten inches and weighed 155 pounds. Never was he known to throw a baseball especially hard. Still, in a career that lasted less than twelve full seasons, John Clarkson would prove to be one of the most effective and impactful pitchers of his age while posting statistics that have endured through the generations since. Respected by some of the best players against whom he played and acknowledged for his tutelage of stars-to-be such as Cy Young, his mark upon the game was definite and distinct, even if it could not have been foreseen.

There is a possibility that John's father was an acquaintance of Harry Wright, who had dropped out of school at the age of fourteen to apprentice to a jeweler, and who had worked for an extended period with Tiffany's, before moving on to the New York Knickerbocker and Cincinnati Red Stockings ballclubs. Thus, John may have learned the game from one of professional baseball's true pioneers. It is certain that Clarkson knew the game by his teenage years, as he played on his high school team, primarily as a catcher. From 1880-1882, he joined the amateur Boston Beacons, developing into both a formidable hitter and pitcher. In doing so, he eventually made contacts amongst the local Boston Red Stockings, receiving tips on how to practice and to maximize his performance. The Beacons had the occasional opportunity to play exhibition games against major league teams, and Clarkson became the beneficiary of one such contest against the

National League Worcester Ruby Legs in April 1882.

John was signed to a major league contract with the Ruby Legs after the game, and he made his major league debut against Boston just a few days later. While he was hit hard in his first game, he contributed two doubles himself and won the game 11-10. However, he lost his next two games and was released just a week into the season after allowing 31 runs, albeit only 12 earned, in 24 innings pitched. The Worcester team folded at the season's end after having won only 18 games. Clarkson joined a Saginaw, Michigan, team in the Northwest League, holding a position as a utility player until his pitching potential was recognized. During that time, John converted to an overhand pitching style, and 1884 saw his first great pitching success as he built a record of 34-9 and a 0.64 earned run average through mid-August, which is when the Saginaw team was forced out of the league for non-payment of dues. As a result, John Clarkson hit the market as a free agent.

Clarkson was pursued by several teams and ultimately signed by Cap Anson's Chicago White Stockings. He lost his first game, which was pitched against Hoss Radbourn, but overall he posted a 10-3 record in 14 games with just a 2.14 earned run average, which was good for sixth place in the league. A control pitcher who relied heavily on curveballs, Clarkson was known for his deceptive delivery. He was even known to wear an over-sized belt buckle in order to distract batters. While his time with the White Stockings was brief in 1884, Clarkson also turned heads by striking out 7.78 batters per 9 innings, a rate that placed him first in major league baseball, comfortably ahead of Jim Whitney's 7.232. Cap Anson purportedly had to learn how to coax the best from his new star pitcher, later noting in an interview that Clarkson had a peculiar temperament and was sensitive to criticism, requiring significant praise and encouragement.

During the subsequent winter, Clarkson began coaching the pitchers of Dartmouth University, and this new winter conditioning, perhaps along with Anson's strategy of praise, brought out his best in 1885. Clarkson completed 68 of the 70 games that he started that season, throwing 623 innings in total. He led the National League in wins (53) and strikeouts (308) while finishing third with a 1.85 earned run average. He was praised by the media for his control and his intelligence as he effectively pitched around dangerous batters. Throughout the season, Clarkson also proved a fun-loving and enjoyable teammate as he and Mike Kelly frequently sang to provide entertainment. Following the season's end, Clarkson posted a 1-1 record with a 1.12 earned run average as his National League Champion White Stockings played in the World Series against the American Association St. Louis Browns. The series ended in a 3-3 tie with a seventh game having been called as a tie because of darkness. There was no World Champion, but Clarkson had established himself as the most valuable pitcher in baseball.

After barnstorming for a few months that winter, John married girlfriend Ella McKenna before again leading Chicago to a pennant in 1886. Clarkson struck out a career-high 313 batters as he posted 36 wins and a 2.41 earned run average in 55 games. Again facing the St. Louis Browns in the World Series, Clarkson posted a 2-2 record with a 2.04 earned run average, but he is best remembered in that series for throwing a wild pitch that provided St. Louis its series-winning victory in game six, an appearance that was Clarkson's fourth game pitched in six days. Compounding the seriousness of the loss were allegations that he had failed to make his planned start in game five because he had been out drinking the night before.

John Clarkson, 1887
Allen & Ginter World's Champions (N28)
Courtesy of Library of Congress PPOC

Clarkson recommitted himself to personal workouts and his Dartmouth coaching position that winter. Entering 1887, he knew that his team would be weakened by the sale of Mike "King" Kelly to Boston, and he would face a new challenge as the official pitching distance had been extended from 50 to 55 feet, 6 inches. However, Clarkson again dominated the league leading all pitchers in wins (38), games (60), complete games (56) and strikeouts (237). Nonetheless, Chicago failed to maintain the dominance it had exerted in the previous two seasons, and the team fell to third place. In addition, whether it was because his family was trying to lure him back to the jewelry business or because he had his own problems with remaining in Chicago, John Clarkson began requesting that he be traded to his Boston home. Chicago wanted $10,000 to part with their ace pitcher, a price that would match the King Kelly deal they had completed the year before, but initial offers from Boston failed to meet that amount. Clarkson refused to sign a contract to play for Chicago, and indeed it looked as though he would not play in 1888 until Boston met the $10,000 asking price on April 3rd and Clarkson rejoined King Kelly as one half of the $20,000 battery.

1888 was a good year, though not a great one. Boston finished in fourth place, and while its new ace led the league with 483.1 innings pitched, he also led the league with 119 bases on balls and finished with a 33-20 record. But any disappointment that Boston fans felt over the $10,000 Clarkson purchase would be quickly eliminated the following year when he would produce one of the most dominant seasons of pitching that major league baseball has ever known.

John Clarkson, 1887-1890
Old Judge (N172)
Courtesy of Library of Congress PPOC

Clarkson began the 1889 season as Boston's temporary team captain, and the team started the season on a hot streak, posting an 18-4 record in May. On June 4th, Clarkson became the first major league pitcher to strike out three batters on nine pitches, and it was clear that he was on his way to having a sensational season. On September 16th, the Beaneaters stood half a game behind the New York Giants and began a 15-game road trip to finish the season. It was agreed that Clarkson would start each of the remaining games, and indeed he did start 13 of the final 15. However, though Clarkson had the best season of his career and shared a roster with future Hall of Famers Hoss Radbourn, King Kelly and Dan Brouthers, Boston fell one game short of the pennant-winning New York Giants as the season was decided on its final day. On the other hand, the second-place finish did nothing to diminish Clarkson's individual performance as he won baseball's pitching triple crown with an amazingly dominant performance. His 49 wins were 11 more than any other pitcher, his 72 games started were 25 more than any other pitcher, his 68 complete games were 22 more than any other pitcher, his 8 shutouts were twice that of any other pitcher, his 284 strikeouts were 59 better than any other pitcher, and his 2.73 earned run average led the league by almost a quarter of a point. In modern terms, his wins above replacement value was the best in the league at 16.2. In 1889, there simply was no better pitcher, and perhaps no better player, than John Clarkson.

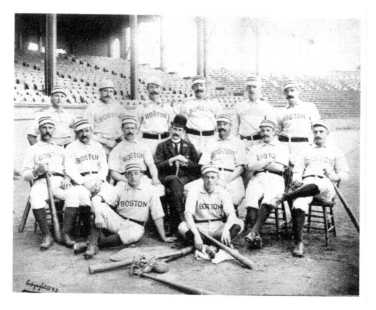

1889 Boston Beaneaters

When the Players' League formed in 1890, though he had previously supported Brotherhood union activity, and though he was one of the initial purchasers of stock in Boston's Players' League team, Clarkson decided not to leave the National League. Instead, he negotiated a previously unheard of $25,000 contract for three years with the Boston Beaneaters. He also agreed to try to recruit more players to the Beaneaters, thereby driving a wedge between himself and players who supported the Players' League and ending many of his close friendships. Even after the Players' League folded, Mike Kelly opted to join the American Association instead of again playing with Clarkson in Boston. Some disgruntled teammates publicly said that they held no ill will, but they were suspected of giving less than their best efforts for Clarkson when he was on the mound. Others treated Clarkson with hostility for the remainder of his career.

Through it all, John Clarkson remained an effective pitcher. After posting a 26-18 record in 1890, he was second in the league in wins with a 33-19 record in 1891 as his Beaneaters finally won the pennant. That season, Clarkson once again finished in the league's top ten in wins, earned run average, games pitched, complete games, shutouts and strikeouts. It would be his last season of greatness.

After he posted an 8-6 record through the end of June in 1892, the Boston Beaneaters released John Clarkson. He was quickly signed as a free agent by the Cleveland Spiders, but he was not expected to be the team's leading pitcher. That spot was already claimed by the young hurler known as Cy Young. Instead, Clarkson entered a supporting role and posted a 17-10 record for Cleveland for the remainder of the season. At season's end, in part because of the velocity of Cy Young, the major league pitching distance was expanded to 60 feet, 6 inches. Facing the second such change in his career, Clarkson's effectiveness suffered. While Clarkson would throw 31 complete games in 1893, that was his lowest season total since he began with Chicago in 1884. His 16-17 record was his first losing record since he went 1-2 with Worcester at the age of 20. Perhaps Clarkson's greatest contribution to the team was his mentorship of Cy Young, who would later acknowledge Clarkson's help in developing his strategy, his curveball, and his control.

Before the 1894 season, Clarkson decided to go on a hunting trip with his good friend and former catcher Charlie Bennett. Tragedy struck when Bennett disembarked a train in Wellsville, Kansas, and then slipped while trying to reboard. As Clarkson watched, Bennett slid under the train's wheels and had both of his legs severed. Clarkson stayed with his friend for more than a month following the accident, and subsequently he organized benefits for Bennett. Clarkson's drinking also increased, and his dissatisfaction in Cleveland grew. He began 1894 with an 8-10 record and a 4.42 earned run average. He pitched his final game for Cleveland in a losing effort on July 12th, and the team traded him to Baltimore the following day.

Clarkson refused to join the Orioles. Instead, at age 32, John Clarkson retired from major league baseball.

Pitching in parts of twelve seasons, Clarkson had posted a career 328-178 record. He completed all but 33 of his 518 career starts, and he posted 1,978 career strikeouts and a 2.81 earned run average in 4,536.1 innings pitched. Clarkson also hit 24 homeruns, by far the highest total for any pitcher of his era, currently tying him for seventh place on the list of all-time homeruns by pitchers.

John Clarkson and his wife opened a cigar store in Bay City, Michigan. They attempted to expand their business enterprises, but they found more challenges than success. John sporadically worked with independent and minor league clubs in Bay City, and he occasionally teased about a potential return to major league baseball. However, in early 1905, as John was preparing to manage Bay City's franchise in the Michigan State League, he had a mental breakdown, and his family had him declared insane. John would remain in asylums and psychiatric hospitals for the next three years. His excessive drinking had seemingly exacerbated depression, paranoia, and various other mental disorders. He retained his physical health and talked vividly about his days in baseball, but he could not connect to his present, and there was little hope for his recovery. While visiting his parents in Winthrop, Massachusetts, in January 1909, John contracted pneumonia that overtook both of his lungs. After being admitted to McLean Hospital, he lapsed into a coma and died at the age of 47.

Major League Debut: May 2, 1882, for the Worcester Ruby Legs

Final Major League Game: July 12, 1894, for the Cleveland Spiders

Win-Loss Record: 328-178

National League Wins Leader: 1896-1898

National League Pitching Triple Crown: 1889

Two 45-win Seasons: 1885 (53) and 1889 (49)

Two Seasons with 600 Innings Pitched: 1885 and 1889

Two 300 Strikeout Seasons: 1885 and 1886

Inducted to the Major League Baseball Hall of Fame: 1963

Clarkson's Hall of Fame Plaque Reads:

> JOHN GIBSON CLARKSON
> WORCESTER, N.L. 1882
> CHICAGO, N.L. 1884-87
> BOSTON, N.L. 1888-92
> CLEVELAND, N.L. 1892-94
> PITCHED 4 TO 0 NO-HIT GAME AGAINST
> PROVIDENCE IN 1885. WON 328 LOST 175
> PCT .652 LED LEAGUE WITH 55 VICTORIES
> IN 1885 (INCLUDING 10 SHUTOUTS) 38 IN
> 1887, 49 IN 1888 AND 49 IN 1889. HAD
> 2013 STRIKEOUTS IN 4514 INNINGS.

ROGER CONNOR

Bonds, Griffey, Aaron, Williams, Ruth.... Each generation has had an opportunity to revisit the title of baseball's Homerun King, sometimes because statistics demand it and sometimes for the healthy sake of inter-generational baseball argument. Through it all, for more than eighty years, Ruth's name has existed as the core of every discussion about the homerun and power hitting, yet as the professional game had existed for decades before Ruth's time, so does the concept of elite power-hitting, though it played a different role in the game. While he never led his league in a single season, consistency, including twelve seasons where he ranked in the top ten in homeruns, made Roger Connor baseball's first Homerun King, a title he held for twenty-four years until he was passed by Ruth on July 18, 1921.

Roger Connor was the third of eleven children, born to Irish immigrants in Waterbury, Connecticut, on July 1, 1857. The *Dred Scott* Supreme Court decision had been issued just months earlier, declaring "separate but equal" to be the law of the land, and Connor's family knew another variation of ethnic prejudice as they lived a life of limited opportunity in the Irish Abrigador district, which was separated from the rest of Waterbury by a granite hill. Waterbury, which would later be home to such baseball notables as Jimmy Piersall and Fay Vincent, is nicknamed the Brass City, and its motto is *Quid Aere Perennius?* (What is more lasting than brass?). Indeed, Connor's father worked at the Waterbury brass works, and Roger would join his father there to provide additional income when he left school at the age of twelve. While Roger loved baseball, his parents did not approve of the game as it distracted from jobs that could help provide much needed income, and Roger was whipped on multiple occasions when his parents found that he had spent a day playing baseball instead of working.

At the age of fourteen, Roger already stood six feet and weighed 180 pounds, and he decided that it was time to set out on his own to find a future in the game he loved. He left his family and moved to New York, working a variety of odd jobs while trying to establish himself with a junior baseball team. Unfortunately, tragedy cut short Roger's opportunity to seek his fortune. His father passed away suddenly in 1874, leaving Roger's mother in economic peril while she tried to provide for his younger siblings. Shouldering the burden of responsibility to his family, Roger left New York's baseball opportunities, and, at the age of seventeen, he returned home to find steady work in Waterbury in order to provide financial assistance to his family while becoming a sort of surrogate father to his brothers and sisters. Roger wouldn't play serious baseball again for two years.

In 1876, he began playing with the semi-professional Waterbury Monitors as a left-handed third baseman. That platform then afforded him the opportunity for a two-week tryout with the minor league New Bedford Whalers, which was a newly formed team in 1878, a tryout where Roger failed to impress as a right-handed batter. He then returned to the Monitors and transitioned to batting left-handed with significantly more success. Roger rapidly made his way into the International Association, which was comprised of two separate Canadian-American baseball leagues, to play for one of New Bedford's rivals. Roger's mother gave her blessing for him to return to the International Association in 1879, where he batted .367, drawing serious attention from other teams.

In 1880, at the age of twenty-two, Roger Connor joined the major leagues, playing for the National League Troy Trojans on a roster that included such notables as Buck Ewing. At more than six feet and two hundred pounds, the Trojans could not provide a uniform for Connor, so they sent him to a shirt factory for individual tailoring. While there, he met a blonde seamstress who he would marry in the fall of the following year and remain devoted to for forty-seven years. Indeed, 1880 proved an extremely successful year for Roger as he ranked third in the league in batting average (.332), fifth in homeruns (3), and third in runs batted in (47) during his first season. The one deficiency that Connor had to face was his fielding. Committing sixty errors in eighty-three games at third base, he would be moved to first base for the majority of his games for the next three seasons.

Roger Connor, 1887-1890
Old Judge (N172)
Courtesy of Library of Congress PPOC

Unfortunately, Roger Connor's sophomore season found his offensive numbers in decline in every significant category. However, his season still featured highlights, specifically his ninth inning at-bat on September 10th against the short-lived Worcester Ruby Legs. In their twelfth and final meeting for the season, Worcester carried a 7-3 lead into the ninth inning. Three Trojan base hits loaded the bases, and, following an out, a base on balls narrowed Worcester's lead to three runs with the bases still loaded. Following a second out, Roger Connor came to the plate as the winning run with the bases loaded and two out in the bottom of the ninth. Connor responded by hitting the National League's first grand slam homerun as a walk-off homerun that delivered a victory to Troy. The next day, *The Troy Times* emphasized the poor pitching and fielding of the day, referring to the grand slam only in its article's final sentence as "the accidental hit of the Megatherian Connor." Still, Connor's homerun, one of two that he hit for the season, secured his power-hitting in baseball's record books for the first time.

In 1882, Connor regained his offensive prowess, leading the league in triples and ranking third in batting average. However, the National League was in flux due to challenges from its new competitor, the American Association, and following the season, the Troy Trojans were dissolved. Connor and nearly half of the dissolved Trojans team were signed by the New York Gothams, a newly formed team that would bring the National League back to New York City for the first time since the end of the 1876 season. Connor responded well to the change, finishing second in the league with a .357 batting average. Furthermore, legend has it that Connor's unusually large size came into play, as it had with his required special uniform fitting in Troy, when he motivated manager Jim Mutrie and others to refer to Connor and other members of the team as Giants, a moniker that would become the team's official name in 1885 and would remain into the twentieth century, even as the team later relocated to San Francisco.

Over the next six seasons with New York, Connor's offensive performance placed him consistently among the league leaders in a variety of categories. He led the league in batting in 1885 (.371), in triples in 1886 (20), and in runs batted in during 1889 (130). In 1886, he even hit a homerun so far that it was first ball to ever leave the old Polo Grounds, impressing the men of the New York Stock Exchange so much that they presented him with a $500 gold watch to commemorate the achievement. Unfortunately, those years also contained the low point of Connor's life when, in 1887, his infant daughter Lulu died of dysentery before being baptized, a tragedy that Connor attributed to punishment for his having married outside of the Catholic Church. However, Connor continued to play, and there were highlights in subsequent seasons, in which the Giants won the 1888 and 1889 National League pennants and participated in post-season play against the pennant winners from the American Association, the St. Louis Browns in 1888 and the Brooklyn Bridegrooms, who would later be renamed the Dodgers, in 1889. The 1888 series was a ten-game series that ranged in attendance from a high of 9,124 at the Polo Grounds for Game 5 to a low of 412 at Sportsman's Park in St. Louis for the inconsequential tenth game. The Giants had clinched a series victory with their sixth win in Game 8, but the series was played through to its conclusion. 1889, the first New York area exclusive post-season, one that began the trans-generational Dodgers-Giants rivalry, featured a best-of-eleven series where it was agreed that the series would end as soon as one team reached a sixth win. Once again, that team was the Giants, who clinched the series in nine games. The 1889 series is also noted as being one of the possible origins of baseball's traditional seventh-inning stretch, as a fan is said to have yelled "stretch for luck" at that point of the game in Game 1. Connor's performance in both post-seasons was significant and consistent. He batted over .300 in both, while hitting for extra-bases, stealing bases and driving in runs (12 in the 9 games of 1889 alone) to help in leading his team to dominance in both series.

Roger Connor, 1887-1890
Old Judge (N172)
Courtesy of Library of Congress PPOC

Unfortunately for the National League Giants, there was a price to be paid for post-season success, and in 1890 that price was the targeting of successful players by the newly formed Players' League. The Players' League formed its own New York Giants team and attracted Connor and other key players to join for what turned out to be a single season. For Connor, who was already being reasonably compensated and who had a good relationship with his owner, the decision to join the Players' League appears to have been an ideological one in which he devoted himself to the labor rights of his fellow players. In the new league, Connor continued to thrive, finishing in the league's top ten for average, triples, runs and runs batted in while leading the league with fourteen homeruns. The Players' League Giants, which featured several future Hall of Famers, finished in third place, and with the demise of the league at season's end, they were purchased by their National League counterparts, which meant a return to the National League Giants for Connor in 1891. It also meant that the Players' League Giants stadium, to be renamed the new Polo Grounds, would be used by the National League Giants for the next sixty-six years, until they moved to San Francisco. Connor further personally benefited in 1890 as he and his wife adopted their daughter Cecilia.

Connor played through the 1891 season with the Giants, but the aftermath of the Players' League break left the team with a significant amount of tension, and Connor decided to break for the Philadelphia Athletics of the American Association for 1892, but before the season began, that team was absorbed into the National League, and he ultimately found himself playing with the Philadelphia Phillies. Connor's continued strong offensive output helped to support the Phillies in a fourth place finish, and with a strong roster, the team looked poised for future success, but Connor was traded back to New York when he refused to sign a contract that would have involved a substantial pay cut.

In 1892, no doubt benefitting from the new league rule that moved the pitcher five feet further from home plate, Connor once again posted strong offensive numbers. His most impressive number, uncovered years later by biographer Roy Kerr, is that, while facing left-handed pitching, Connor hit four of his eleven homeruns for the season while batting right-handed. However, the Giants were not competitive for the pennant, and Connor was ultimately released early in the 1894 season in favor of a youth movement. He played the remainder of his major league seasons with the St. Louis Browns, which had entered the National League after the American Association's bankruptcy in 1891. Connor's years in St. Louis were difficult ones as the team failed to achieve. The 1896 season allowed Connor a brief and unsuccessful stint as player-manager, one that he did not enjoy because he was uncomfortable in challenging umpires' decisions. Nonetheless, his offensive numbers remained respectable, and his defensive performance had become much improved from his early playing years. The team's low point occurred during Connor's final season in 1897 when the Browns finished with a 29-102 record, which would stand as an all-time franchise low. Connor was not significantly associated with the dismal finish, as he had been released by the team in May.

For the next six years, Roger Connor worked in the minor leagues as a player, manager, and owner. In keeping with his personality, he became known for protecting umpires from local crowds rather than arguing their decisions. June 1902 featured Connor's first and only ejection in professional baseball as he physically fought with an opposing player who had thrown his brother to the ground. Connor's career ended with a .275 performance in 1903 at the age of forty-four, a season in which he was finally forced to wear eyeglasses. Baseball had become a family affair in the years since he left the minor leagues as his wife, daughter and brother worked alongside him in various capacities until his 1903 retirement, upon which he began a second career as a school inspector in his hometown.

As Ruth approached and passed Connor's homerun record in 1921, Connor was retiring from that second career as a maintenance worker for the Waterbury public schools. He lived outside of public and media discussion, and he was not even mentioned by the news coverage of Ruth's 139th career homerun, which generally wasn't even recognized as being a record at the time. He was even laid to rest in a grave that remained unmarked from his death in 1931 until 2001. At the time of his death, however, his local paper wrote that Connor's "likeable personality and his colorful action made him an idol." Nonetheless, it would be decades before Connor's name resurfaced in mainstream discussion of Major League Baseball, as Hank Aaron's assault on Ruth's career record invited a revisiting of homerun history. What is evidenced in Connor's career numbers is that, like Ruth and Aaron, Roger Connor was not a one-dimensional player only notable for his power. He batted for a high average, captured a batting title and competed for others in the course of his career. He also featured speed on the bases, stealing 244 bases and ranking fifth on the all-time list with 233 triples. Without question, he was more than a player whose homerun record was later surpassed by others – he was a player of exceptional ability and performance, worthy of being known as one of baseball's all-time greats.

Professional Debut: May 01, 1880, for the Troy Trojans

Final Major League Game: May 18, 1897, for the St. Louis Browns

Career Batting Average: .317; led league in 1885

4-time NL Batting Champion: .317 in 1879, .381 in 1881, .347 in 1887
    and .344 in 1888

Career Hits: 2,467; led league in 1885

Career Homeruns: 138

Career RBI: 1,322; led league in 1889

Inducted to the Major League Baseball Hall of Fame: 1976

Connor's Hall of Fame Plaque Reads:

> ROGER CONNOR
> TROY N.L., NEW YORK N.L.,
> NEW YORK P.L., PHILADELPHIA N.L.,
> ST. LOUIS N.L. 1880-1897
> POWER-HITTING STAR OF DEAD BALL ERA.
> SET CAREER HOMERUN RECORD FOR 19TH
> CENTURY PLAYERS. WON LEAGUE BATTING
> CHAMPIONSHIP IN 1885 AND HIT .300 OR
> BETTER 12 TIMES. HIT THREE HOMERS
> IN A GAME IN 1888 AND MADE SIX HITS IN
> SIX AT-BATS IN A GAME IN 1895.

ED DELAHANTY

On July 9, 1902, a male body wearing only tie, shoes and socks, mangled and missing one leg, was found in the river at the lower Niagara gorge. The body was promptly identified by family members as that of Ed Delahanty, the 35 year-old superstar outfielder for the Washington Senators, less than a season removed from a batting title, who had been missing since July 2, when he tried to illegally walk across the International Railway Bridge towards Buffalo, NY, and instead fell into the Niagara River after scuffling with a night watchman. The tragedy occurred at the end of a week of bizarre, and sometimes violent, behavior as Delahanty attempted to abandon his American League Senators in order to jump to John McGraw's New York Giants. Many questions remain about the final moments of Delahanty's life, but, for many, Delahanty's deadly fall into the Niagara while he still possessed remarkable skill and fame would eclipse the actual career accomplishments of one of the best hitters in baseball history. The larger-than-life slugger was proven to be tragically mortal.

Edward James Delahanty was a first generation American, born October 20, 1867, the eldest surviving child of two Irish immigrants who had settled in Cleveland, Ohio. 1867 was a year of pioneering as it also was the birth year of Wilbur Wright, Laura Ingalls Wilder, Frank Lloyd Wright and Scott Joplin, as well as being the year that the United States purchased the territory of Alaska in a deal that was then known as Seward's Folly. The Civil War was over, and the country had turned its focus upon growth and reconstruction. The Delahanty family also dedicated itself to hard work and growth. Ed would also eventually be the eldest of five brothers, a group of siblings unique in American history in that all five brothers spent time in the major leagues during their baseball careers. According to Ed: "We were given bats instead of rattles." The accomplishment doubtlessly grew from the brothers' early childhood of playing a tremendous amount of sports, activity which kept them out of their house during the day, as their mother had converted the home to a boarding house in order to supplement their father's blue-collar income.

Ed was also able to contribute to the family income once he was invited to play with the semi-pro Cleveland Shamrocks baseball club, in addition to beginning his own blue-collar work around Cleveland. But he was soon offered fifty dollars a month to play with Mansfield, Ohio, in the Ohio State League in 1887. Ed made a quick decision, but it could not have been an easy one. According to Tommy Leach, who grew up in Cleveland with Delahanty and was later also a major leaguer, Ed didn't go home after accepting the Mansfield offer, thereby avoiding his parents and leaving immediately. His parents were upset and wanted to bring him home to work, though Ed was already nineteen years old. Instead, the Delahantys let their son try his hand at professional baseball, and that year, while Ed reportedly batted .351 while scoring 90 runs in 83 games, another Irish baseball player, Mike "King" Kelly, was the talk of baseball in America as the Boston Beaneaters purchased his contract for an unimaginable $10,000 after he had led the league in hitting in 1886. Kelly, a showman, went on to tour San Francisco in 1887, a trip that possibly inspired Ernest Thayer's authorship of "Casey at the Bat", which rapidly became famous, possibly providing Ed a literary model of the greatness that could be achieved by a powerful Irishman in the American game. Ed wouldn't have to wait long for his chance at stardom. After batting .412 in twenty-one games in Wheeling, West Virginia, to begin 1888, his contract was purchased, for $2000, by the Philadelphia Quakers of the National League.

Playing in the newly constructed state-of-the-art Philadelphia Base Ball Grounds, later known as Baker Bowl, Ed initially struggled in the major leagues, batting only .228 in 1888. Though his batting improved to .293 the following season, he still saw only very limited playing time with a total of 261 plate appearances. Perhaps in an attempt to gain more playing time or to revitalize his seemingly stalling career, when the Players' League formed for the 1890 season, Ed decided to join them, jumping to the Cleveland Infants of his native state, where he would prove his skill by batting .296 over a full season of regular playing time. When the Players' League folded after its single season, he returned to the Philadelphia National League team, which was operating under a new official name: the Philadelphia Phillies. Delahanty readjusted to the National League in 1891, but his season was mediocre at best. Thereafter, Delahanty devoted himself to exercise and physical fitness, returning in 1892 in much better condition, and he led the league in triples and slugging while batting above .300 for the first time and driving in 91 runs.

It is also in July 1892 that Delahanty also supposedly suffered perhaps the greatest humiliation of his baseball career. Legend has it that, in the eighth inning of a game in Philadelphia, Cap Anson came to bat and hit a fly ball that supposedly struck a pole and ricocheted towards right field. The scoreboard was in the right field wall, and there was a small building in front of the wall used to house the scoreboard numbers. The ball somehow bounced into the storage building, which looked like a doghouse, and Ed Delahanty found himself stuck when he tried to reach into the building in order to retrieve the ball, leaving only his flailing legs visible to the Philadelphia crowd. Anson circled the bases for a homerun before Hall of Fame teammate Sam Thompson managed to pull Delahanty and the ball from the doghouse. If true, the story would account for Anson's single homerun of 1892, but the play would have led to no significant damage as the Phillies did not lose a home game to Anson's Colts during July 1892, instead beating the Colts in both meetings at the Baker Bowl.

Ed Delahanty, 1887-1890
Old Judge (N172)
Courtesy of Library of Congress PPOC

In 1893, Ed Delahanty led the league in homeruns and runs batted in, and from there his accomplishments only grew during his remaining nine seasons in Philadelphia. He would become the first major league player to bat over .400 three times, winning a batting title in 1899 with an average of .410. Perhaps more unbelievably, in 1894 Delahanty was part of a Phillies outfield which saw all four players bat better than .400 for the season (Tuck

Turner at .416, Thompson and Delahanty at .407, and Billy Hamilton at .404), though none of them was able to secure the batting title. In all, during his time with the Phillies, in addition to his batting title, Delahanty led the league in doubles four times, triples once, homeruns twice, and runs batted in three times (never driving in less than 91 in a season after 1891). In 1896, he also managed to break up a Cy Young no-hitter with two outs in the ninth. Interestingly, many of Delahanty's best years occurred from 1896-1899, the same years as the Klondike Gold Rush that arose from the much-maligned Alaskan Purchase that occurred the year of his birth.

Beyond being an offensive force respected throughout the major leagues, Delahanty was also able to run, field and throw. He compiled 456 stolen bases throughout his career, including a league-leading 58 in 1898. His hustle also translated to great defensive play in the outfield, and his strong throwing arm earned him 238 career assists, ranking him twenty-seventh on the all-time list. Like Thayer's Mighty Casey, Delahanty had become a fan favorite, a powerful hitter who could dominate the game, a skilled Irishman whom the crowd could count upon to deliver time and time again. Nonetheless, Delahanty's Phillies never won a pennant, with their best finish that of second place in 1901. Ed became frustrated with his salary, which had risen only $200 over his eight straight .300 or better seasons, and that he felt, at approximately $3000 per year, did not satisfactorily reflect his performance on the field or his value to the team. In the immediate sense, that meant that Delahanty would test the waters of the American League, which had its inaugural season in 1901. In 1902, Delahanty was quoted as saying, "I know I am getting along in years and won't be able to last much longer in first-class baseball, therefore I am going to get all the money there is in sight... Last year I was playing with the Phillies for $3,000, this season the Washington Club gives me $4,000, and if I can get $5,000 no one can blame me for taking it." In fact, not only did Delahanty leave the Phillies to join the Washington Senators in 1902, he also became one of the American League's best recruiters, influencing nine other players from the 1901 Phillies team to make the jump to the American League the following year.

The American League was quickly impacted by Delahanty's skill and bat. In his initial season with the Senators, he led the league in batting and doubles, while batting in 93 runs. Almost 120 years later, he remains the only player to win batting titles in both the National and American Leagues. Still, Washington finished in sixth place, and Delahanty began to face a number of immediate challenges.

Ed's gambling began to drain his resources, and at the same time, his wife became quite ill. When the couple's financial problems were seemingly solved with a substantial contract with the New York Giants valued at $6,000-$8,000 per season with a $4,000 advance, the Delahanty's fell victim to peace between the American and National Leagues. The Leagues agreed to honor each other's contracts, thereby killing the Delahanty deal among others, and they recognized one another to the extent that League champions were able to face off in the first World Series in 1903. Further complicating matters, Delahanty was required to return New York's $4,000 advance, which was already spent, and the Washington Senators had already advanced him money on his 1903 salary as well. In desperation, he held out until Washington agreed to repay the money that Delahanty owed New York, but they required restitution that guaranteed his financial problems to continue into the future. As a result, a troubled and overwhelmed Delahanty found himself returning to a Washington Senators team in 1903 that was destined to finish last in the league both in terms of their record and their attendance.

Ed drank heavily and continued to gamble. He reportedly begged teammates for financial support and threatened suicide when they would not provide it. It is believed that Delahanty attempted suicide on at least one occasion by turning on the gas in his room in Washington. He began giving away keepsakes and took out a life insurance policy. His behavior had a negative impact on his playing condition, and while he maintained a .333 batting average during 42 games through June 25, 1903, his power numbers and runs batted in were greatly reduced, and he was not able to play every day. His hope continued to be to jump to another team, perhaps in the Western League, that would provide him a new, lucrative contract.

Then, in late June, National League President Harry Pulliam allowed George Davis to jump from an American League team to play for the New York Giants, and Delahanty once again saw the possibility to escape to better economic circumstances. Delahanty continued to drink heavily, and once again threatened to kill himself. When teammates attempted to intervene, he chased them through the team hotel with a knife. Ed was convinced to travel with the Senators to Detroit, where his mother and two of his brothers planned to meet him to help calm the situation. However, the draw of the New York possibility proved to be too much as Delahanty was desperate to see his ill wife and to provide financial stability. He left the Senators in Detroit and boarded a train to New York City.

While on the train, Ed Delahanty drank five whiskeys. He became disorderly, damaged property, and tried to pull a young woman from her berth by her ankles. When others tried to intervene, Delahanty brandished a straight razor in an effort to hold them back, and the conductor gathered help to confront him. At the time, the train was in Canada, and Canadian policy required the conductor to deliver unruly passengers to a constable, but the conductor did not do so. After all, the passenger in question was Ed Delahanty. Instead, because something had to be done, Delahanty was removed from the train at Bridgeburg, on the Canadian side of the border, and he was specifically warned to not cause further trouble because he was still in Canada. Reportedly Delahanty replied, "I don't care whether I'm in

Canada or dead."

Delahanty then proceeded to the International Railway Bridge, which stretched to Buffalo, NY, and did not allow for passengers, Delahanty decided to cross. He was intercepted by a night watchman and the two struggled. Delahanty managed to force his way past and continued, though the draw of the bridge was open to allow for a boat. It is unclear, at that point, whether Delahanty jumped or if he stumbled, but he ultimately fell to his death in the Niagara River. His body would not be recovered for almost a week, about twenty miles downstream. While foul play was suspected by some, none was ever proven.

Almost a century after Ed's death, author and historian Bill James would be quoted as asserting "Joe DiMaggio is the closest replica to Del I have ever seen. His every move is taken from the same baseball mold as Ed Delahanty." Hall of Fame teammate Phil Rizzuto would say of DiMaggio, "There was an aura about him. He walked like no one else walked. He did things so easily. He was immaculate in everything he did. Kings of State wanted to meet him and be with him. He carried himself so well. He could fit in any place in the world." While those words may also possibly be applied to Ed Delahanty the baseball player, a great a powerful talent who dominated the game and became the envy of others in and around the sport, unfortunately they cannot be transferred to Ed Delahanty the man. Instead, *New York Times* sportswriter Robert Smith wrote of Delahanty, "Men who met Ed Delahanty had to admit he was a handsome fellow, although there was an air about him that indicated he was a roughneck at heart and no man to temper with. He had that wide-eyed, half-smiling, ready-for-anything look that is characteristic of a certain type of Irishman. He had a towering impatience, too, and a taste for liquor and excitement. He created plenty of excitement for opponents and spectators when he laid his tremendous bat against a pitch."

With a batting average of .3458, Delahanty ranks fifth best in major league baseball history. If his legacy were not dominated by the nature of his early death, he might largely be considered one of the best right-handed hitters the game has ever known. Instead of being a success, his story as a first-generation American is a tragedy. Still a dominant force in the game, he lost his life in terrible circumstances. Like the Mighty Casey, a larger-than-life superstar batsman of amazing skill, Big Ed Delahanty ultimately proved to be human, to be flawed.

Major League Debut: May 22, 1888, for the Philadelphia Quakers

Final Major League Game: June 25, 1903, for the Washington Senators

Career Batting Average: .346; led league 1899, 1902

Career Hits: 2,596

Career Runs Batted In: 1,464; led league 1893, 1896, 1899

Inducted to the Major League Baseball Hall of Fame: 1945

Delahanty's Hall of Fame Plaque Reads:

ED DELAHANTY
ONE OF THE GAME'S GREATEST SLUGGERS.
LED NATIONAL LEAGUE HITTERS IN
1899 WITH AN AVERAGE OF .408 FOR
PHILADELPHIA; AMERICAN LEAGUE
BATTERS IN 1902 WITH A MARK OF .376
FOR WASHINGTON, MADE 6 HITS IN 6
TIMES AT BAT TWICE DURING CAREER
AND ONCE HIT 4 HOME RUNS IN A GAME.

HUGH DUFFY

In 1941, as Ted Williams pursued a .400 batting average for the season, he sought advice from a white-haired, energetic figure who had been with the ballclub for more than twenty years as a manager, scout, front office official, instructor and coach. Hugh Duffy was seventy-four years old that season, but he worked with Williams and effusively praised the young star's skills: "I think he has a wonderful chance to top my record. I can say this about Teddy – I have never seen a better hitter than Williams in all of my life…" The record of which Duffy spoke was his own .440 batting average achieved in the 1894 baseball season – the highest single season batting average in baseball history. "You've got to be lucky," Duffy said. "The year before I hit .440, I had an average of something like .380, and I'm sure that I hit the ball better that year than the next one when I made the record. I tell that to some people and they think I'm daffy, but honest, it's the truth." Perhaps it was Duffy's own humility that prevented him, for many years, as being recognized as one of baseball's all-time greats, or perhaps it was a general unawareness of the sport as it had existed in the 1890s, but his record .440 average has stood for 125 years and may perhaps never be challenged.

Hugh Duffy's exact birth date and place are the subject of some disagreement, but research has uncovered a baptismal record for Hugh Duffy, son of Michael and Margaret Duffy, dated November 28, 1866, for a church in Cranston, Rhode Island. Most biographies assume that his date of birth had been two days earlier. Hugh was raised with two sisters in a small, close Irish family. Though he would later claim to have completed two years of high school, census records indicate that he began working sometime between the ages of 9 and 13. While Duffy would mature to a height of just five feet, seven inches, the physical labor of his young life certainly left their mark on his broad shoulders, powerful upper-body and strong wrists. At the same time, his recreation came in playing baseball in the local sandlots.

In 1884, the year following his mother's death, 18-year-old Duffy began playing semi-pro baseball, playing catcher for the River Point team for the salary of five dollars per week. The next year, he moved to Jewett City, Connecticut, and began playing for thirty dollars per week plus room and board for the company team of the linen dye factory where he had found employment. In 1886, Duffy moved another 75 miles to play for a factory team in Winsted, with his salary climbing to fifty dollars a week plus room and board, a significant figure considering that the average Connecticut laborer at that time earned two dollars per day with a sixty-hour work week. Months later, Duffy debuted professionally, playing for the Eastern League Hartford Dark Blues. Playing catcher and second base, he batted .278 in seven games before the season's end.

1887 saw Duffy prove his skill in a variety of settings as he played for three teams over the course of the season, the first two each succumbing to unfavorable financial realities. After batting .350 in seventeen games with the Eastern League Springfield Horsemen, he moved to the New England League's Salem Fairies, for whom he batted .461 over twenty-seven games. Thereafter, his addition to the New England League Lowell Lions helped to drive the team to the league's pennant as he batted .475 while scoring 71 runs in forty-nine games. More importantly, Duffy had become the target of major league interest, and he was able to negotiate his season's performance into a $2000 contract with the Chicago White Stockings who had finished in third place in the National League for Cap Anson that same year.

Famously, when Duffy reported to Anson, his underwhelming 5'7" frame prompted Anson to remark that the team was not in need of a batboy. Anson did not approve of Duffy's size, his ethnicity or his Catholic faith, and the rookie spent the next two months watching his teammates from the bench. Only when Marty Sullivan, the team's replacement for one-time star and future evangelist Billy Sunday, proved inadequate did Duffy get an opportunity. He had two hits in six at-bats in his June 23, 1888, debut. The performance apparently met with Anson's approval as Duffy remained in the lineup and, by season's end, he had played in 71 games, primarily in right field, batting .282 with 7 homeruns and 41 runs batted in. The Chicago team finished in second place.

Hugh Duffy, 1887-1890
Old Judge (N172)
Courtesy of Library of Congress PPOC

Having proven himself the previous season, Hugh Duffy played in all 136 of Chicago's 1889 games, leading the league with 584 at-bats. His batting also improved to a .312 average with 12 homeruns (5th in the League), 89 runs batted in (9th in the League), and 52 stolen bases (7th in the League). Another difference of opinion between Duffy and Anson was realized, however, when Duffy decided to leave the Chicago White Stockings for the newly formed Players' League Chicago Pirates for the 1890 season. Anson, at that point a shareholder in the Chicago National team, heavily criticized those who left the league for the rival player-owned enterprise, and the two would never play on the same team again. Still, while the Players' League would last only a single season, it provided Duffy with his break-out campaign as he led the league in hits (191), runs (161) and at-bats (596) while amassing a .320 average with 7 homeruns, 82 runs batted in and 72 stolen bases. At season's end, as the Players' League folded for lack of funding, the Chicago Pirates were bought out by Anson's National League Colts, but Duffy refused to return to Anson's team.

Instead, Duffy negotiated a contract with the National League

Boston Beaneaters, but that agreement was blocked by the Chicago team's assertion of the National Agreement that provided the terms for which Players Association players would be reintegrated into the National League. In this case, Duffy could only return to the League through Anson's Colts. Instead, he opted to sign with the Boston Reds of the American Association, which had denounced the National Agreement in early 1891. Alongside teammates King Kelly and Dan Brouthers, Duffy batted .336 while leading the league with 110 runs batted in for the season. Duffy also met outfielder Tommy McCarthy while playing with the Reds, and the two would share the outfield, a business and a strong friendship for years to come. The Reds won the American Association pennant, but the team folded at season's end as the American Association dissolved following the defection of several of its teams to the National League. Baseball, however, was likely not at the forefront of Duffy's mind as he married Katherine Gilland in October 1891.

As he looked to return to the diamond, with the demise of both the Player's League and the American Association, the National League remained Duffy's only viable option for a continued career in baseball, but his season with Boston had removed him from the control of Anson's Colts. Instead, he signed with the Boston Beaneaters, with whom he would play the next nine seasons, including those that would be the most prolific of his career. Tommy McCarthy also signed with the Beaneaters, continuing the relationship that would become known as that of the "Heavenly Twins." Duffy's Beaneater career began solidly, but relatively quietly, as he hit .301 with 5 homeruns and 81 runs batted in during the 1892 campaign, but those numbers increased to a league-leading .363 average with 6 homeruns 147 runs scored, and 118 runs batted in for 1893. The team won the National League Pennant in each season. Duffy distinguished himself by batting .462 with a homerun and 9 runs batted in during the 1892 series, but there was no postseason series in 1893.

The 1894 season found the Beaneaters without a pennant for the first time in four years as the team fell to third place. However, Duffy's performance soared to provide one of the greatest single-season batting demonstrations of all-time, but the season began as one marred by personal tragedy. Katherine had been overcome with consumption, and concerns over her health were serious. Duffy declined financially lucrative exhibition opportunities following the 1893 season in order to spend the winter with Katherine on the west coast, hopeful that the warmer climate would strengthen her. As they returned to Massachusetts to prepare for the upcoming season, Katherine succumbed to the disease. She was removed from her train and hospitalized in Blackstone, Massachusetts, but she could not be saved. Katherine Gilland Duffy died on March 31, 1894, at the age of 25.

Perhaps baseball provided an escape from Duffy's grief. He began the 1894 season late, ultimately playing in 125 of the Beaneater's 132 games, his lowest games played total since his rookie season, but he attacked the ball with a skill that resulted in a .440 average while he also led the league with 237 hits, 51 doubles, 18 homeruns and 374 total bases. He also scored 160 runs, stole 48 bases and hit 16 triples, missing the league's triple crown only because he finished second in runs batted in (145 to Sam Thompson's 149). Adding to the difficulty of the season had been the burning down of the Beaneaters' South End Grounds on May 15th, leaving them to play in the former home of the Boston Reds until their home field could be rebuilt two months later. Still, falling in line with Duffy's sensational hitting, the 1894 Boston Beaneaters scored 1,220 runs for the season, which remains a Major League Baseball record.

Duffy followed his greatest season with another excellent one in 1895. He batted .353 with 9 homeruns, 100 runs batted in, 112 runs scored

Hugh Duffy, 1909-1911
T-206
Courtesy of Library of Congress PPOC

and 42 stolen bases. Duffy also remarried to Nora Moore at the season's end. While her moral perspective required him to leave his business partnership with Tommy McCarthy in their Boston saloon, the Heavenly Twins remained good friends, and Duffy's marriage to Nora would be a happy one for the next 57 years.

1896 was more difficult as Duffy's batting average dropped to .300 and his runs scored to 97, both totals were his lowest since his rookie season. While he did contribute 113 runs batted in, the Beaneaters finished 17 games behind the league leaders, and Duffy's good friend Tommy McCarthy was sold to the Brooklyn Bridegrooms. Still, Duffy was in his prime, and he returned for his age 30 season in 1897 with great success, batting .340 and leading the league with 11 homeruns. He also scored 130 runs, batted in 129 and stole 41 bases. As a revitalized Hugh Duffy returned to prominence, so did the Boston Beaneaters. The team won the pennant for the first time in three years, and while they lost the post-season Temple cup to the Baltimore Orioles, they retained a reputation for being one of the greatest teams of the nineteenth century. Duffy hit a dominant .524 with 7 runs batted in for the series.

Boston won the pennant again in 1898, their fifth of the decade, as the United States entered and won the Spanish-American War. While a good portion of the offense was contributed by future Hall-of-Famers Jimmy Collins and Billy Hamilton, Hugh Duffy contributed a .298 average with 97 runs scored and 108 runs batted in. There was no 1898 postseason, as the Temple Cup series had ended its four-year existence as a postseason playoff series the year before, and no replacement would come until the 1900 Chronicle-Telegraph Cup.

Duffy's numbers declined again in 1899, though they remained respectable at .279 with 5 homeruns, and 103 runs scored. His 102 runs batted in marked the last of seven consecutive seasons in which he batted in 100 or more. As the century turned, the 33-year-old Duffy was able to play in only 55 games. While he batted .304, he was not capable of the consistent play or the offensive production for which he had become known. After nine seasons with the Boston Beaneaters, Duffy's National League career drew to a close, and he began to survey baseball for the offer of a new opportunity.

He quickly found that opportunity in Milwaukee, the city where Ban Johnson founded the American League, a former minor league that removed itself from baseball's National Agreement, which was the formal arrangement between the National League and baseball's minor leagues. Johnson announced the American League as a direct competitor to the National League only two months later, signaling the American League's beginning as a major league, earning it the nickname "the Junior Circuit" as the National League had already been long established. As one of the new league's eight charter franchises, the Milwaukee Brewers were in need of a manager, and Duffy took the job, bringing with him a tremendous amount of baseball experience. Unfortunately, Duffy also proved to be the Brewers' best player, batting .302 with 2 homeruns and 45 runs batted in. After a heart-breaking

14-13 loss to the Detroit Tigers on opening day, in which the Brewers surrendered nine runs in the ninth inning, the team went on to finish with a 48-89 record. At the season's end, the team was relocated to St. Louis, where it would become the St. Louis Browns, but Duffy did not go with them, instead deciding to remain in Milwaukee.

For the next two seasons, Hugh Duffy served as player-manager for the Milwaukee Creams of the Western League. As he gained leadership experience, he also found success, leading the Creams to a third-place 80-54 record in 1902 before winning the 1903 pennant with an 83-49 record. Such success drew the attention of Major League Baseball, and Duffy accepted a managerial position with the National League Philadelphia Phillies beginning in 1904.

The Philadelphia Phillies team of which Duffy took charge was not a good one. They finished the 1904 season with a 52-100 record, 53.5 games behind the New York Giants. Playing sparingly, Duffy batted .283 with 5 runs batted in and 10 runs scored in 59 plate appearances. 1905 found Duffy playing even less, batting .300 in 41 at-bats, but he was able to turn around the Phillies' team performance dramatically as they finished in fourth place with an 83-69 record. While the team's record fell to 71-82 in 1906, they again achieved a fourth-place finish. Team ownership parted ways with Duffy at the season's end. Duffy's major league playing career also drew to a close with a single hitless at-bat in 1906. Including his brief play with the Phillies, Duffy batted .326 over parts of 17 seasons. He finished his career with 2,293 hits, 325 doubles, 119 triples, 106 homeruns, 1,554 runs scored, 1,302 runs batted in, and 574 stolen bases. He was 39 years old.

After doing more than a respectable job as manager and part owner of the Providence Grays of the Eastern League over three seasons, Duffy was given a chance to manage again in the majors with the Chicago White Sox. Duffy had been White Sox owner Charles Comiskey's teammate on the 1890 Chicago Pirates, but Duffy only retained his manager's position for two years despite their friendship and moderate success for the team. He spent the next several years managing in different major league locations with results ranging from a losing season with the American Association Milwaukee Brewers in 1912 to winning a pennant with the Portland Duffs of the New England League in 1915. The Great War later brought an opportunity to join the coaching staff at Harvard, and in 1920 he moved again to the International League Toronto Maple Leafs, where his team posted a 108-46 record.

Winning allowed Duffy yet another chance to return to the Major Leagues, as he joined the Boston Red Sox in 1921. It was a team far removed from its talented 1918 World Championship roster, and it was still reeling from the sale of sensation Babe Ruth just two years before. Under Duffy's management, the Red Sox posted consecutive losing seasons, and he was transitioned into a scouting and coaching role beginning in 1923. Over the next thirty years, Duffy continued to instruct and influence baseball players at the major league level. The single distasteful episode of that stage of Duffy's career was one that he could not control: Boston's 1945 farce of a tryout for Jackie Robinson, Sam Jethroe and Marvin Williams, Negro League ballplayers striving to integrate baseball for the first time since Cap Anson influenced the exclusion of African-American players in 1883. While Duffy merely ran the tryout and had no known impact on its outcome, the Red Sox handled the situation badly and, along with most Major League teams of the period, ended up on the wrong side of integration history.

Duffy's ultimate retirement finally came in 1953, as President Truman was leaving the White House and the Korean War was finding resolution through an armistice. When Duffy had begun his major league career, Harry Truman had just celebrated his fourth birthday, and Korea was still governed by the Joseon Dynasty that had been in place since the late-14th-century. While he was still alert and impactful in his instruction, Duffy's wife of 57 years, Nora, had died, and he was ill and suffering from prostate cancer.

Hugh Duffy was elected to the Baseball Hall of Fame by the Veteran's Committee in 1945, but he did not attend that, nor any other, induction ceremony. While in his lifetime, Duffy's single-season batting record was thought to stand at .438, the statistic immortalized on his Hall of Fame plaque, a reevaluation of box scores from that season has led to the corrected statistic of .440, a mark that will likely never again be reached in the Major Leagues, a mark that stands as the defining characteristic of Hugh Duffy's long and incredibly successful career.

Major League Debut: June 23, 1888, for the Chicago White Stockings

Final Major League Game: April 13, 1906, for the Philadelphia Phillies

Career Batting Average: .326; led league 1893-1894

Career Hits: 2,293

Career Homeruns: 106; led league 1894, 1897

Career Runs Batted In: 1.302

Career Stolen Bases: 574

Triple Crown: 1894

Inducted to the Major League Baseball Hall of Fame: 1945

Duffy's Hall of Fame Plaque Reads:

> HUGH DUFFY
> BRILLIANT AS A DEFENSIVE OUTFIELDER
> FOR THE BOSTON NATIONALS, HE
> COMPILED A BATTING AVERAGE IN 1894
> WHICH WAS NOT TO BE CHALLENGED
> IN HIS LIFETIME - .438.

WILLIAM "BUCK" EWING

A baseball player's ability cannot be entirely represented in numbers. In the 1919 *Reach Baseball Official Guide*, sportswriter Francis Richter wrote of Buck Ewing as follows: "It is a difficult, not to say ungrateful, task to select any one player as superior to all the rest, though we have always been inclined to consider catcher-manager William (Buck) Ewing in his prime, from 1884 to 1890, as the greatest player of the game. From the standpoint of supreme excellence in all departments – batting, catching, fielding, base running, throwing and base ball brains – a player without a weakness of any kind, physical, mental, or temperamental [sic]." Twenty years later, Ewing became the first catcher admitted into the Baseball Hall of Fame, thereby cementing his legend for the ages. During the following year, the *Official Baseball Guide* wrote, "William (Buck) Ewing is considered by many to have been the greatest all-around player who ever lived. Some go even further and rate Buck... the best ballplayer of all time." Yet, while the annals of baseball history heap such superlative praise upon Ewing's play, a casual reading of his statistics may not seem to warrant it. Ewing led his league only once in triples and once in homeruns. His highest batting average for a full season was .344, with his career average finishing at .303, both of which are admirable numbers, but they have been far surpassed many times. In fact, in terms of career offensive statistics, Ewing only ranks in the top twenty in a single category, coming in eighteenth in career triples with 178, a number surpassed by several of his contemporaries. In short, Ewing's reputation is founded not only upon his success, but also upon the manner in which he achieved it. The nature of his play, his baseball intelligence, and the manner in which he revolutionized the game may not easily be embodied in numbers, but they were readily apparent to those who saw him play. Those men would later not hesitate to give Ewing top ranking, even after the days of Cobb, Wagner and Ruth, leaving little doubt about the elite level of his skill.

Buck Ewing's origins virtually overlap with the origins of professional baseball. He was born in Hoagland, Ohio, on October 17, 1859, and his family moved to Pendleton, Ohio, a suburb of Cincinnati, when he was two. Little is known about Buck Ewing's childhood, but he would have been just shy of seven years old when the Cincinnati Base Ball Club formed in June of 1866. The club began as a strong regional amateur team that went 16-1 before beginning to rely increasingly on player imports from eastern cities for the following season. In 1869, the National Association of Base Ball Players, the first organization governing American baseball, issued new rules allowing for a professional category of teams, and the Cincinnati team became the Cincinnati Red Stockings, America's first openly professional baseball team. The 1869 Red Stockings were without precedent. They placed ten men on salary for an eight-month period and proceeded to travel across the country, taking on challengers everywhere from San Francisco to Boston. They finished the season with an undefeated 65-0 record, and they were a national sensation, finding themselves memorialized in lithographs and print publications such as *Harper's Weekly*. Surely nine-year-old Buck Ewing was captivated by the team that put his hometown on America's baseball map as he played baseball in the fields of Cincinnati that summer.

In his teens, Ewing worked for the Cincinnati distiller Meddux & Hobart as a delivery driver for their product within the Cincinnati area. The job allowed him to have Sundays free to play baseball, though there is confusion as to whether Buck was playing for the local amateur Mohawk club or the semi-professional Cincinnati Buckeyes when he was signed in 1879 by Horace Phillips, of the Rochester National Association team, for $85 a month. In 1880, Ewing began playing baseball professionally, batting only .148 in fourteen games for Rochester before being moved to the National League Troy Trojans. Ewing caught his first game as a major leaguer on September 9, in what turned out to be a frustrating 1-0 loss, and he proceeded to bat just .178 in thirteen total games for the season. Nonetheless, Troy stuck with its young catcher, and Ewing showed significant improvement in the next two seasons, batting .250 in 67 games in 1881 and .271 in 74 games in 1882. At the end of the 1882 season, the Troy Trojans, along with the Worcester Worcesters, were disbanded because the National League deemed the two cities too small to support their teams. Worcester actually hosted the Trojans for the final two games of the season. The penultimate game had six fans in attendance, the lowest total ever at a major league game, and the final game hosted just twenty-five. At season's end, Buck Ewing was in search of a new team.

Ewing looked to return home to Cincinnati for the 1883 season, signing a contract with the Cincinnati Reds of the American Association. However, when the newly formed New York Gothams took Troy's slot in the National League, as part of a joint agreement between the National

League, the Northwestern League and the American Association, the Gothams were granted rights to several former Trojans, including Ewing, Roger Connor, and Mickey Welch. Though the deal was not of Ewing's doing, some Cincinnati sportswriters began to criticize him for reneging on the deal that would have returned him to his hometown. Nonetheless, the deal was made and the Gothams soon became known as the New York Giants, and they played to a 46-50 sixth place finish in their inaugural season. Ewing's performance continued to improve as his batting average topped .300 for the first time. His versatility also became apparent as he played second base, third base, shortstop and outfield in addition to his primary position as catcher. Perhaps most notably, Ewing also led the league with ten homeruns, which is a tremendous number considering that his teammates combined for a total of twelve, including just one by Roger Connor, who would go on to hold the career homerun record for decades.

Buck Ewing, 1887-1890
Old Judge (N172)
Courtesy of Library of Congress PPOC

Although he primarily served as a catcher throughout the 1880s, Ewing played all nine positions at various points in his career, some of them with regularity. While some of his critics asserted that this was because he wasn't defensively strong enough to hold down a regular position, most of his contemporaries praised his defense as a catcher, leading to the belief that Ewing played other positions because of the toll that catching took upon his body. That position is persuasive considering that Ewing was one of the first catchers to crouch immediately behind the batter, rather than fielding the position by standing several feet behind home plate, as did most catchers of the day. Ewing also helped to innovate the equipment tied to the position, including the catcher's mask and chest protector, as well as being one of the first to switch to a padded pillow-type catcher's mitt instead of an unpadded glove. He further innovated the position by using his foot to block home plate, dropping his mask in such a way as to obstruct runners' paths to the plate, and throwing out would-be base stealers with snap throws from his crouch. He also served as a leader to his team on the field as Hall of Fame teammate Mickey Welch asserted that he never shook off a pitch that Ewing called for, and that Ewing, during his time with the Giants, originated the pre-game clubhouse meeting in order to provide a strategy for the coming contest and to motivate his team. However, Ewing's service as a catcher was severely curtailed after the 1890 season, during which he caught 81 of the 83 games in which he played while batting .338. Playing catcher in an 1891 exhibition game, he injured his arm while attempting to throw out a runner stealing second base. The injury was so severe that Ewing was limited to just fourteen games during the 1891 season, and catcher would never again be his primary position.

Frustrated with their inability to achieve team success, the New York Giants installed Ewing as team captain in the midst of the 1887 season. In that era, a team's captain would assign defensive positions, make the batting order, coach baserunners, and have the responsibility of being the team's spokesperson to the umpires. Ewing replaced shortstop John Montgomery Ward as captain because of team frustration about Ward's relationships with the other players, including Ewing, though Ward remained with the team. The team finished with a winning record, but they could not move above fourth place. However, the next season was a different story. With a roster of star players and Ewing's leadership, the Giants won their first pennant in 1888, finishing nine games ahead of the second place Chicago White Stockings. Interestingly, during the season the Giants used a relief pitcher on only two occasions, and on both occasions that pitcher was Buck Ewing, who pitched a total of seven innings with a 2.57 earned run average. Following the season, New York was offered a playoff series against the St. Louis Browns for the World Championship. New York won the series six games to four, and Ewing batted .346 in the process.

During the 1889 season, New York once again achieved the pennant, although this time by a narrow margin of just a single game over the Boston Beaneaters. Ewing also had a sensational season, batting .327 with 87 runs batted in, 91 runs scored and 34 stolen bases. He even started two games as pitcher that season, achieving complete game victories on both occasions. In the 1889 World Series, the Giants faced the Brooklyn Bridegrooms in the first series between these two teams that would later evolve into the tense Giants-Dodgers rivalry. The Giants won the best-of-eleven series six games to three, therein achieving back-to-back championships. The 1889 championship was also Ewing's last.

Buck Ewing, 1888-1889
Old Judge (N173)
Courtesy of Library of Congress PPOC

1890 saw the baseball labor movement boldly undertake the creation of a Players' League, and Buck Ewing was one of many baseball stars to leave his former team to support this new effort. Ewing was actually a difficult figure for the player's effort, which was focused on a need for better wages, as his salary had increased from $1000 in 1881 to $5000 for the 1889 season, an incredibly high amount for the period. Still, he secured a position as player-manager for the New York Giants of the Players' League, not to be confused with the National League New York Giants which existed in the same season.

While Ewing managed his Giants to a third-place finish, and while he individually distinguished himself on the field by ranking in the league's top ten for batting average, slugging percentage, triples and homeruns, his reputation amongst other players began to suffer for the first time. This problem of reputation seems to have arisen from Ewing's failure to separate himself sufficiently from his old club, as he was seen meeting socially with National League New York Giants' players and ownership throughout the season. The situation further escalated when, during the Players' League's single season, Ewing himself acknowledged that Aaron Stern, the owner of the Cincinnati Reds through 1889, had once offered him $8000 to leave the Brotherhood of Professional Baseball Players, baseball's first effort towards a labor union. When the Players' League failed to survive into 1891, many were left to wonder whether leaders like Ewing had done enough or whether they were controlled by outside interests.

In 1891, Ewing returned to his captaincy of the National League Giants, but he could not return to his former stature. Ewing was frustrated at the Players' League's failure, and that frustration was only compounded by his arm injury, which limited him to just fourteen games for the season. Several of Ewing's teammates thought that Ewing could have played more often, that his arm injury was simply an excuse. Some felt that he sat out because he begrudged the National League, and others felt that he had lost his nerve as a catcher, especially as the Giants had been joined by hard-throwing Amos Rusie. Ewing's .347 batting average in the fourteen games that he did play did little to support the legitimacy of his injury. Finally, and perhaps most importantly, Ewing took on a central role in the season's pennant race between the Boston Beaneaters and Cap Anson's Chicago Colts. In a late season five-game series against the Beaneaters, Ewing was accused of convincing the Giants' manager to let most of his regulars sit out so that Boston would have an edge and be able to move ahead of the Colts in the standings. Ewing's supposed motivation was resentment towards Anson for not supporting the Players' League, thereby perhaps contributing to its failure. Later, Ewing was further accused of providing New York's team signs to the Boston team in order to give the Beaneaters a further edge. Finally, Ewing indicated that when he did return to the Giants full-time, he believed it would be best for him to play first base in order to minimize his throwing. As a result, established first baseman Roger Connor left the Giants for the Philadelphia Phillies, and Ewing's image suffered even further.

Ewing played the majority of his 1892 games at first base, and he performed well at the plate, once again landing in the league's top ten for batting average, slugging percentage, triples and homeruns. Still, his time in New York had come to an end. The Giants finished in eighth place, a disappointing 71-80. There also appeared to be no way to heal the friction that existed between Ewing and his teammates, so the Giants decided to trade

Ewing to the Cleveland Spiders in early 1893. At the time, that trade was viewed as a one-sided act of charity by the Cleveland team to return the favor for league support that had kept the Spiders afloat for the previous few seasons. Humbled and seeking to reestablish himself, Ewing responded with his best major league season, batting .344 while scoring 117 runs, batting in 122 runs, and stealing 47 bases. However, for the Spiders, it was a step backwards as they won twenty games fewer than they had in the previous season, slipping from a second-place finish to third. In 1894, the Spiders fell even further in the standings, finishing in sixth place, and Ewing was not able to provide any substantial offensive contribution. He played in only 53 games, and all of his offensive statistics fell significantly. He was released in July.

Once again, Buck Ewing was able to reestablish himself, signing with the Cincinnati Reds as a player-manager. His offensive numbers returned in 1895, as he batted .318 with 90 runs and 94 runs batted in, but his playing time reduced significantly in 1896 and ended altogether after he appeared in a single game in 1897. Ewing would continue to manage the Reds from 1895 to 1899, posting a winning record in each season. However, Ewing's time as manager was not considered successful. During 1896, as his team appeared headed towards claiming a spot in the post-season, other clubs began to rest and save their best pitchers to face Ewing's team, targeting him for defeat as a way to repay him for the Players' League failure and his role in fixing the outcome of the 1891 season. His own team began to accuse him of playing favorites, of being unable to motivate his team, of using poor strategy, and of cheating in order to win, such as when he had an umpire locked in the Cincinnati dressing room in mid-1896 in an effort to get a substitute umpire that was more likely to favor his team. As the years passed, his relationship with players, ownership and the media continued to deteriorate, and he was fired in December 1899.

Ewing signed to manage the New York Giants in 1900, but he was not able to hold the position for long. The Giants lost 42 of their first 63 games, and Ewing was fired in late July. He had neither the goodwill nor the winning record to continue. Instead, Buck Ewing retired from professional baseball. He returned to Cincinnati, where he opened a baseball school and profited from real estate investments. He passed away at the age of 47 on October 20, 1906.

During the course of his career, Buck Ewing was clearly a skilled player. From the time that he joined the Gothams in 1883, Ewing regularly batted above .300. He led the league in triples (1884) and homeruns (1883), and if one excuses the 1891 season when he played only fourteen games, from the time stolen base statistics were kept beginning in 1886, Ewing averaged 35 stolen bases a season. He also revolutionized the catching position, captained two world championship teams, and had a successful managerial career. However, those facts do not serve as the basis of Ewing's legacy or his Hall of Fame admission. Instead, his legacy is established because his contemporaries largely considered him to be the best catcher, and perhaps the best player, ever to play the game of baseball, an assertion not based upon statistics, but rather upon the manner in which he played the game. The poor relationships and troubled reputation that Ewing suffered for the last decade of his career now serve him as evidence that the praise he received must have been objective and well-earned. For those who saw him play, Buck Ewing was simply one of the best.

Professional Debut: September 09, 1880, for the Troy Trojans

Final Major League Game: May 27, 1897, for the Cincinnati Reds

Career Batting Average: .303

Career Triples: 178

Career Homeruns: 71; National League Leader in 1883

Career Runs Scored: 1,129

Career Managerial Record: 489-395

Inducted to the Major League Baseball Hall of Fame: 1939

Ewing's Hall of Fame Plaque Reads:

> WM. B. "BUCK" EWING
> GREATEST 19TH CENTURY CATCHER. GIANT
> IN STATURE AND GIANT CAPTAIN OF
> NEW YORK'S FIRST NATIONAL LEAGUE
> CHAMPIONS 1888 AND 1889. WAS GENIUS
> AS FIELD LEADER, UNSURPASSED IN
> THROWING TO BASES, GREAT LONG-RANGE
> HITTER. NATIONAL LEAGUE CAREER
> 1881 TO 1899 TROY, N.Y. GIANTS AND
> CLEVELAND; CINCINNATI MANAGER.

WILLIAM ROBERT "SLIDING BILLY" HAMILTON

Winning in baseball simply involves scoring more runs than the opposing team, and with 1697 runs scored in only 1594 career games, no one in baseball history has been as effective at scoring runs as Billy Hamilton. Still, Hamilton is not a well-known figure. In his 1999 *New Historical Baseball Abstract*, Bill James writes that, "Hamilton was completely invisible in the literature of the sport up to 1960 and was not elected to the Hall of Fame until 1961. He left no legend behind him, no stories, no anecdotes..." Such an explanation may seem odd as Hamilton lived until 1940, well past many of his contemporaries, and he was active in baseball until 1917, well past his major league playing days. He was even awarded a lifetime pass to National League baseball games in 1936 based on his lifetime service to the game. Still, his major league career was relatively short, as he played over the course of just fourteen seasons, but his statistics are spectacular, even when put into the context of the era in which he played. While it is true that Hamilton played under a different set of rules than today's players, and that does make it difficult to directly translate his performance to the modern era, consideration of his playing record clearly established him as one of the most impactful players to ever play the game.

William Hamilton was born in Newark, New Jersey, on February 16, 1866, a year in U.S. history with a reputation for theft as it was also the year of the Jesse James Gang's first robbery, the first daytime bank robbery in the United States, and it was the birth year of famed outlaw Butch Cassidy. The first child of Irish immigrants Samuel and Mary Hamilton would eventually be memorialized in baseball's record books for his ability to steal bases, a play that had just originated in 1865 when Ned Cuthbert stole the first base in organized baseball while playing for the Philadelphia Keystones.

Little is known about Hamilton's childhood. His sister Mary was born two years after him, and within two years after that, the Hamilton family moved to Clinton, MA, where his father found work in a textile mill. As Billy was growing up, he would have witnessed the opening of the Clinton Public Library in 1873, and he would have spent time at Fuller Field, which opened in 1878 and is now the world's oldest continuously used baseball field. Billy grew to a height of only 5'6", but, having been a sprinter in school, his legs were powerful, allowing him incredible speed both on the bases and in the outfield. As a result, throughout his teens, Billy was able to compete professionally with semi-pro teams. Still, while Billy yearned for an opportunity to play baseball professionally, when he left school in his early teens, it was to join his father in the textile factory.

It seems that Billy got his first chance to play professional baseball in 1887, when he joined the Lawrence team of the New England League that had formed the year before, with teams in Massachusetts and Maine. Using the name Robert Hamilton, he played 87 games at first base and only a single game in the outfield. He batted .393 with 22 doubles and 89 runs, but the team struggled with a 44-50 record, and they were moved to Salem in mid-July to finish the season. Returning much closer to home, Billy joined the league's Worcester Grays for 1888. With the Grays, Billy played all 61 of his games in the outfield, and his offensive production continued as he batted .351, scored 76 runs, and stole 72 bases. As impressive as his numbers are, they constitute only a partial season of play as Worcester sold Billy to the Kansas City Cowboys of the American Association in July, a necessary decision as the New England League was on its way to being inactive for the next two seasons.

Billy Hamilton made his major league debut with the Cowboys on July 31, 1888, on the losing end of a no-hitter by Philadelphia Athletics' pitcher Gus Weyhing. Unfortunately, that experience was indicative of what was to come that season, as the Cowboys continued to a 43-89 record that was the worst in the major leagues. Still, Hamilton batted .264 in his thirty-five games with the club, earning himself a spot as the regular right fielder for the following season. 1889 didn't offer much more success for the Kansas City club as they finished seventh of eight teams with a 55-82 record, but Hamilton continued to establish himself with a .301 batting average, 144 runs scored, and a league-leading 111 stolen bases. It is important to note that modern stolen base rules were not implemented until 1898, so for much of Hamilton's career stolen bases were credited when a runner reached an extra base upon a hit by another player. Furthermore, catchers did not play immediately behind the batter, and pitchers were largely not practiced in holding runners on base. However, the stolen base was an important part of the game. As Harold Seymour wrote in his *Baseball: The Early Years*, the attitude of the time was that "[a]ny soft-brained heavy weight could hit a home run, but skill on the bases required shrewdness and intelligence." Thus, Hamilton proved himself intelligent on the bases by any measure as his 111 stolen bases were twenty more than the number of second place finisher Darby O'Brien. Hamilton's play placed him in demand as the Cowboys team dissolved due to its lack of success, and his contract was sold to the Philadelphia Phillies for $5000.

Billy Hamilton, 1887-1890
Old Judge (N172)
Courtesy of Library of Congress PPOC

Like most other teams, the Phillies, who were rebranding themselves after having been known as the Quakers in previous seasons, were fielding new players in 1890 as the newly formed Players' League had prompted several defections. Hamilton was installed in left field, and he responded with another fine season, batting .325 with 133 runs scored and a league-leading 102 stolen bases. On the other hand, Hamilton had trouble in the field. He made more errors than any other National League outfielder with 34, having trouble both with catching the ball and with making throws in to the infield. Nonetheless, he had his first taste of winning in the major leagues as the Phillies finished in third place with a record of 78-53. Unfortunately, that would be Philadelphia's best finish during Hamilton's time with the club until the team finished with an identical 78-53 record for another third-place finish in 1895, his final year with the Phillies.

Though they wouldn't compete for the pennant, the 1891 Phillies assembled what would be their outfield alignment for the next several seasons as Hamilton and teammate Sam Thompson were joined by Ed Delahanty, who was returning to Philadelphia from his season in the Players' League. Hamilton was a defensive liability once again as he finished second in the National League with 31 errors, but he more than made up for his fielding mishaps with his best offensive season to date. Billy Hamilton led the National League in hits (179), batting average (.340), walks (102), runs scored (142) and stolen bases (111), aiding Thompson and Delahanty as they each finished in the league's top ten for runs batted in. In the following season, Hamilton's stolen base total dropped to 57, which was still sixth in the league, but he was consistent with his earlier performances by delivering 183 hits, a .330 average and 132 runs scored. Still, Hamilton's best performances lay in the seasons ahead of him.

An 1893 rules change moved the pitcher five feet further from home plate, to the modern distance of sixty feet, six inches, in an effort to increase the game's offense. That spring, under the new rule, Billy Hamilton became the first major league player to achieve a very rare and exciting feat. Entering the season with ten career homeruns, he faced the Washington Senator's Smiling Al Maul on May 17th. Returning to the major leagues after having spent the 1892 season playing in the Eastern League and working in his family's grocery store, Maul faced Hamilton as the leadoff batter in the bottom of the first and quickly surrendered a leadoff homerun. Nine innings later, Hamilton faced Maul again in the bottom of the 10th, and the result was another homerun, a two-run walk-off, establishing Hamilton as the first player to hit both a leadoff and a walk-off homerun in the same major league game. 1893 seemed full of such success, and in August, Hamilton held a .380 batting average and a .490 on base percentage, both of which would ultimately lead the league. However, his season was cut short on August 10th with a diagnosis of typhoid fever. The Phillies slipped from second place to fourth, leaving them to look forward to a fresh start the following season.

While 1894 would ultimately bring another Phillies fourth place finish, it also brought Philadelphia the best offensive season by a team's outfield in major league baseball history. As the team's leadoff man, Hamilton had returned to prime form. In his finest season, with 225 hits and 128 bases on balls, he batted .403 and led the league with a .521 on base percentage and 100 stolen bases. Incredibly, over the course of the season, Sam Thompson batted .415, Ed Delahanty batted .404, and substitute outfielder Tuck Turner batted .416, each contributing to Hamilton scoring 198 runs for the season, which still remains the all-time single-season record. Hamilton's outfield defense also improved as he cut his number of errors in half from previous seasons, committing only 15. Unfortunately, the improved defense could not be maintained as he once again committed 31 errors in the 1895 season, but his stellar offensive production remained a constant as he again led the league in walks (96), stolen bases (97) and runs (166), while batting .389. Nonetheless, 1895 would be Hamilton's last season in Philadelphia. He was traded to the Boston Beaneaters for third baseman Billy Nash on November 14th.

In 1896, Hamilton took over as the leadoff batter and center fielder for the Beaneaters. In addition to continuing his production by batting .366 while once again leading the league in on base percentage (.478) and walks (110), Hamilton was also able to enjoy playing in Boston because it allowed him to return home to Clinton, MA, on a regular basis as Clinton was only an hour from Boston by train. He had married a Clinton girl in 1888, and he and his wife were able to settle their four daughters there with Billy coming home regularly for off-days during the season. After settling into his new city and his new team, Hamilton was able to turn his attention to something that had eluded him throughout his career to that point: winning a pennant.

With Billy Hamilton and teammate Hugh Duffy leading the way offensively and Kid Nichols acting as the ace of the pitching staff, the Beaneaters scored the most runs in the league and allowed the fewest, building a record of 93-39. Still, the race to the pennant was a close one with the Baltimore Orioles finishing only two games behind the Beaneaters over the course of the season. In the final week of the season, the two teams met for three games with only half of a game separating them in the standings. The teams split the first two games before a Baltimore law preventing baseball on Sunday delayed the series' final game until Monday, September 27. A crowd of about 30,000 fans tore down a portion of the fence and overwhelmed the turnstiles to get access to the contest that would decide the season. Kid Nichols pitched for Boston on two days' rest, and scoring was frequent for both teams until Boston secured the lead on the way to a 19-10 victory. Boston found itself a game and a half ahead of Baltimore with just three more to play on the season's schedule. For his part, Billy Hamilton had four hits, three runs and two stolen bases on his way to a season that saw him bat .343 while leading the league with 105 walks and 152 runs scored. The season's end brought more baseball as the Boston Beaneaters faced off against their nemesis from Baltimore again for the Temple Cup series that would determine the 1897 champions. Baltimore, who had played for the Temple Cup in each of its four years in existence, won the series 4 games to 1. But in having defeated Baltimore for the pennant, Boston had become a team of significance in the National League.

1898 offered the challenge of change. As the Spanish American War caused the United States to emerge into global affairs, Major League Baseball introduced a new stolen base rule, and Billy Hamilton was playing on a team that was defending their pennant. Of course, a new stolen base rule challenged one area of Hamilton's statistical dominance. Not counting the 1893 season that had ended early for him due to typhoid fever, Hamilton had averaged 99.13 stolen bases since 1889, his first full season, including five seasons in which he led the league. Those numbers included every occasion in which Hamilton was able to take an extra base for his team, but beginning in 1898, a stolen base would only be awarded if a runner achieved an extra base through his own effort, without the benefit of a hit or an error. As a result, Hamilton's stolen base numbers were reduced, but not significantly, as he still stole 54 bases, which placed him second in the National League at age 32. Likewise, defending the pennant proved manageable. Hamilton batted .369 while scoring 110 runs and leading the league with a .480 on base percentage, and the Beaneaters led the league with a 102-47 record. With the Temple Cup series discontinued due to lack of fan interest, the Boston Beaneaters ended the season as champions.

Injuries began to take their toll on Hamilton in 1899, limiting him to only 84 games as the Beaneaters fell to a second-place finish. In 1900, he returned for a full season, finishing on the league's top ten for hits (173), walks (107), batting average (.333) and on base percentage (.449), but the window for team success seemed to have closed as Boston sank even further in the standings, ultimately landing in fourth place with a 66-72 record. The stolen base was no longer a dominant part of Hamilton's game as he stole only 32 bases in 1899, his career low for a full season. The 1901 season would be his last. With the American League open as a new major league alternative, many players were shifting teams, but Hamilton stayed with Boston. He played in only 102 games, and he posted a .287 batting average and 20 stolen bases, his lowest marks in both categories since 1888, when he played the first 35 games of his major league career for Kansas City.

After his major league career was over, Billy Hamilton continued in baseball. He became player-manager of the Haverhill, MA, New England League team. He began playing full-time again in 1904, when he led the league in batting average, stolen bases and runs while leading his team to the pennant. He then moved about in the Tri-State League and the New England League for the next six years, winning one more batting title before retiring as a player in 1910. He scouted for Boston for the next two seasons before returning to the New England League to manage for three more. His final activity in baseball came as he bought an interest in the Eastern League's Worcester team in 1916, surely remembering that his own playing time in Worcester had served as his stepping-stone to the majors almost thirty years earlier. He sold that interest in 1917, leaving baseball entirely for a position as a production foreman in a Worcester manufacturing plant. He retired in the early 1930s, battled heart disease, and passed away in Worcester on

December 16, 1940.

While Hamilton's statistics were incredible in each season that he played, baseball placed little emphasis on career statistics at the time, sadly allowing Hamilton's totals to pass unappreciated. However, conditions were considerably different a generation later when Ty Cobb's fierce play led to his career total of 897 stolen bases, a figure highlighted as Cobb became part of baseball's first Hall of Fame class in 1936. The following year, Hamilton wrote to *The Sporting News* in defense of his own numbers: "I was and will be the greatest base stealer of all time. I stole over 100 bases on many years and if they ever re-count the record I will get my just reward." At the end of his playing career, Hamilton's stolen base total stood at 937, but when the number was eventually recalculated in line with the game's modern rules, his total still stood at 914. Still, when Lou Brock ended his career as a base stealer, he made sure that his final stolen base was number 938, safely honoring Hamilton's legacy.

Major League Debut: July 31, 1888, for the Kansas City Cowboys

Final Major League Game: September 16, 1901, for the Boston
Beaneaters

Career Batting Average: .344; League Batting Champion: 1891 and 1893

Career On-Base Percentage: .455; League Leader 1891, 1893, 1894, 1896,
1898

Career Stolen Bases: 914; League Leader 1889-1891, 1894, 1895

Career Runs Scored: 1,697; League Leader 1891, 1894, 1895, 1897

Inducted to the Major League Baseball Hall of Fame: 1961

Hamilton's Hall of Fame Plaque Reads:

> WILLIAM R. HAMILTON
> PHILADELPHIA N.L. 1890-1895
> BOSTON N.L. 1896-1901
> HOLDS RECORDS FOR SINGLE SEASON:
> RUNS SCORED, 196 IN 1894; STOLEN
> BASES, 115 IN 1891. LIFETIME TOTAL
> STOLEN BASES, 937. BATTED .395 IN
> 1893, .399 IN 1894, .393 IN 1895.
> LED NATIONAL LEAGUE IN 1891 WITH
> .338 AVERAGE. LIFETIME BATTING
> AVERAGE OF .344. SCORED 100 OR
> MORE RUNS DURING 10 SEASONS.

WILLIAM HENRY "WEE WILLIE" KEELER

Willie Keeler embodied the concept that baseball is a game accessible to men of any size. At five feet, four inches, he was one of the smallest regular players in major league history, but in the eyes of many who saw him play, he was perhaps the greatest batsman the game has ever known. Over a nineteen-year career, he posted nearly 3,000 hits, including eight consecutive seasons with more than 200 hits, and he finished his career with a .341 batting average. In the words of fellow Hall of Famer Sam Crawford, "He choked up on the bat so far he only used about half of it, and then he'd just peck at the ball. Just a little snap swing and he'd punch the ball over the infield. You couldn't strike him out. He always hit the ball somewhere." Indeed, Keeler's consistent success suggested that he found hitting to be as simple a matter as his famous mantra implied: "Keep your eye clear and hit 'em where they ain't; that's all."

Keeler's life began like countless others of his time: as the son of hardworking New York Irish immigrants who had come to America to make a better life. His father, William Henry O'Kelleher, adopting the name Pat Keleher, took work as a trolley switchman on the DeKalb Avenue Line in Brooklyn, married Mary Kiley, and purchased a home in the neighborhood of Bedford. The couple had five children, the eldest three of which survived to adulthood. Willie, born March 3, 1872, was the middle child.

Willie grew up playing baseball, served as the captain of his high school team as a freshman, and then he dropped out of school the following year at the age of fifteen to take a paid position on a local factory team though he didn't work at the factory. His father, probably hoping to provide some sense of responsibility and a viable future, secured a job for Willie at a different factory. Willie worked for a week, earning two dollars, and then earned three dollars at a Saturday baseball game. He never returned to the factory, instead playing for a variety of semipro teams in New York and New

Jersey using the name Willie Keeler. For the remainder of his life, the closest he would come to traditional work came when he sold programs for Brooklyn's Ward's Wonders of the 1890 Players' League. Instead, Keeler devoted himself to baseball, and throughout his teens, his skill, particularly with the bat, continued to develop. In 1891, while pitching and playing third base, Keeler led the Central New Jersey League in batting as his team won a championship. The following year, he was signed to his first professional contract by the Binghampton team of the Eastern League. Keeler won another batting title, thereby offsetting the fact that he committed 48 errors in 93 games, and he drew the attention of several major league teams. On 27 September, he was signed by the New York Giants, beginning a major league playing career that lasted more than eighteen seasons. Debuting at the age of 20, while Keeler was able to play only 14 major league games in 1892, he certainly proved to be in his element from the start as he finished the season with a .321 batting average.

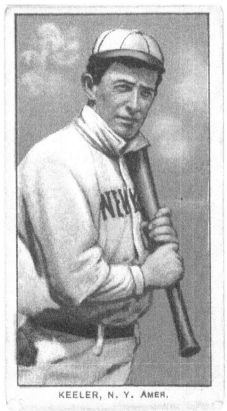

KEELER, N. Y. AMER.

Willie Keeler, 1909-1911
T-206
Courtesy of Library of Congress PPOC

Keeler began 1893 with the Giants and performed well, earning 8 hits in 24 at-bats including two doubles, a triple and an inside-the-park homerun. However, on the day following his homerun, Keeler fractured his leg while sliding into second base, and he missed the next eight weeks of the season. By the time he was ready to return, he had lost his position, and he was traded to the Brooklyn Grooms with whom he would play 20 games. He failed to finish the season at the major league level because of his poor fielding which resulted in 10 errors in just 12 games at third base with Brooklyn. Instead, he was returned to the minor leagues where he committed 11 more errors in 15 games. Still, his overall major league batting performance was strong with a .317 average, two homeruns and 16 runs batted in during a season of just 27 games.

1894 would be Keeler's breakout year as he played more than 125 games and recorded more than 500 at-bats for the first of thirteen consecutive seasons. On January 1, Keeler and Dan Brouthers were sent from Brooklyn's organization to the Baltimore Orioles, and in addition to achieving personal success, they would contribute to the development of one of baseball's first dynasties. Keeler was moved to the outfield, thereby removing the pressure from his defense, and, more importantly, he was introduced to the Baltimore Chop, a strategy of deliberately driving a ball down into the dirt and using speed to beat out the resulting high hop for a hit. When combined with Keeler's bat control and his ability to bunt, the Baltimore Chop made him a lethal adversary. Teammate John McGraw observed, "It was impossible to play for him. I have seen the outfield come in behind the infield or the infielders close up till you'd think you couldn't have dropped the ball into an open spot if you had it in your hand – but Keeler would invariably punch a base hit in there somewhere." Keeler's first Baltimore season ended with 219 hits for a .371 batting average in addition to 94 runs batted in and 165 runs scored. Baltimore won its first pennant, after having finished in eighth place the previous season, though the season's success was somewhat curtailed when they were swept in baseball's first postseason Temple Cup series, four games to none, by the New York Giants.

Keeler's 1895 season was almost a carbon copy of 1894. He belted 213 hits for a .377 average while driving in 78 runs and scoring 162. The Baltimore Orioles won another pennant, but they again lost the Temple Cup series, this time four games to one against the Cleveland Spiders. One notable new development in 1895 was that the nickname "Wee Willie" had begun to appear in newspapers throughout the country.

1896 brought the Baltimore Orioles another league pennant and the team's first Temple Cup championship as they swept the Spiders in a four-game series. Keeler was, once again, one of the team's offensive leaders with 210 hits for a .386 batting average, 82 runs batted in, 153 runs scored, and what would be a career-high 67 stolen bases. However, rather than serving as the peak of Keeler's career, 1896 was a taste of further greatness that would come the following year. In 1897, Keeler opened the season with hits in his first 44 games, breaking the previous record of hits in 42 consecutive games by Bill Dahlen of the 1894 Chicago Colts. With the hit that he logged in his final 1896 game, Keeler had officially hit in 45 straight, a major league record that would stand until Joe Dimaggio's 1941 56-game streak, and a National League record that never been eclipsed. While Keeler's hitting streak was snapped, his dominance for the season was not. He finished the campaign with a league-leading 239 hits and a career-best .424 batting average, an average that soared above second-place finisher Fred Clarke's admirable .390. Baltimore fell two games short of winning its fourth consecutive pennant, though they tied their previous season's mark of 90 victories, but the team did win its second Temple Cup series, this time four games to one over the Boston Beaneaters. Keeler continued his offensive tear through the Temple Cup series with a .471 postseason batting average.

Even with all of his success, Willie Keeler had his frustrations in 1897. His fielding in the outfield drew repeated criticism from John McGraw, and eventually their confrontations boiled over into a naked fistfight in the team's shower room. Nonetheless, since moving into the outfield, Keeler had established himself as a competent fielder. Steve Brodie, the team's center fielder, attested, "He knew his territory like a child its ABC's." Indeed, even McGraw would have to admit that a June 1898 barehanded catch that Keeler made against Washington was the greatest fielding play that he ever saw.

In 1898, Keeler posted only 7 doubles, 2 triples, 1 homerun, 44 runs batted in and 28 stolen bases, significant reductions from his performance in other seasons. However, he led the league with both 216 hits and a .385 batting average while scoring 126 runs, proving that he was still unquestionably an elite player. The Orioles won an impressive 96 games, but that still left them in second place behind the Beaneaters. There was no postseason to be played as the Temple Cup series was ended due to a lack of fan interest, which was blamed upon the purported frustration that the second-best team in season competition had won the Cup in three of its four years of competition. As a result, the 10-8 loss that Baltimore suffered on October 15th to finalize its season record at 96-53 was the team's final game in 1898. It was also the final game that Willie Keeler would play for the Baltimore Orioles.

Almost simultaneous to the 1898 Spanish-American War marking the emergence of America into global affairs, the beginning of the 1899 season marked the end of the Baltimore Orioles dynasty that had begun five years earlier. During the offseason, the Baltimore Orioles and the Brooklyn Bridegrooms had consolidated ownership groups. Unlike the Orioles, the Bridegrooms had not recently been competitive, having most recently completed 1898 in tenth place with a 54-91 record. As a result, ownership decided to move some of the Orioles stars to the Brooklyn team, which was being renamed the Superbas, hoping to achieve a balance that would allow both teams to find success. Keeler was glad to accept the change of assignments, especially because it would allow him to be closer to his mother who was in poor health. When asked about the change by the *Brooklyn Eagle*, he responded, "I can say frankly that I would rather play in Brooklyn, my home, than anywhere else."

Willie Keeler, 1911
Turkey Red Cabinets (T3)
Courtesy of Library of Congress PPOC

Unphased by the change in teams, Keeler kept hitting. With 216 hits and a .379 batting average, he propelled the Superbas while leading the league with 140 runs scored. His single homerun of the year was his career's only grand slam. Brooklyn won the pennant with 101 victories, six more than the second-place Boston Beaneaters and 15 more than the fourth-place

Baltimore Orioles. At season's end, the Baltimore Orioles were dissolved as part of a restructuring that reduced the major leagues from twelve teams to eight. Despite the changes, the Superbas maintained their dominance, winning the 1900 pennant by four and a half games. Keeler led the league with 206 hits while finishing fourth with a .362 batting average along with 41 stolen bases, 68 runs batted in, and 106 runs scored.

In 1901, a new major league, the American League, began competition and attempted to draw talent from the National League to build fan interest. At least six of the eight American League teams sought to sign Keeler, with the Detroit Tigers allegedly offering him $5000 per season, more than double the $2400 salary cap imposed by the National League. However, it was the reformed Baltimore Orioles under the new leadership of John McGraw that most concerned Brooklyn's ownership. Despite their occasional differences, Keeler and McGraw had actually maintained a strong friendship, and Keeler would actually serve as an usher at McGraw's 1902 wedding. As Keeler began to demand a raise in salary, the media identified Baltimore as the team most likely to draw his interest, and the Superbas undertook an effort to raise $1000 in donations to keep Keeler with his hometown team. While the Superbas were able to retain Keeler, they lost several other key players, and they ultimately finished 1901 in third place. Keeler maintained his greatness with 202 hits, a .339 batting average and 123 runs scored.

In 1902, Keeler maintained his position in the league's top ten in several offensive categories including second in hits with 186, third in batting average at .333, and eighth in runs scored with 86. However, those numbers each represented a ten-year low in his performance. Clearly, as he aged and his skills dulled ever so slightly, Keeler benefited from the reduction of National League talent due to the competition of the American League. Similarly, while the Brooklyn Superbas finished in second place in 1902, the truth was that they were no longer a strong major league competitor because the talent loss to the American League had left the National League with a competitive imbalance. In winning its second consecutive pennant in 1902, the Pittsburgh Pirates won the season by an astounding twenty-seven and a half games while leading the league in every significant offensive category. Surely recognizing this reality, as he traveled to California for an off-season barnstorming tour, Keeler visited American League president Ban Johnson to ask whether the American League would be placing a team in New York. Upon learning that the Baltimore Orioles were being relocated to New York to become the Highlanders, Keeler signed an $11,000 contract to play for them, thereby moving to the American League and becoming baseball's first player to earn more than $10,000 a year.

During the subsequent offseason, a horse-drawn buggy in which Keeler was traveling overturned, injuring his leg and throwing shoulder. Still, while commuting from Brooklyn, Keeler played 132 games for the Manhattan-based New York Highlanders in 1903. With 160 hits, he batted .313 and scored 95 runs. The reduction in Keeler's offensive numbers didn't create alarm – it was actually in line with a general reduction in offense throughout the league caused by a new rule that began counting foul balls as strikes against batters. The rule, allegedly adopted because of Keeler's known strategy of fouling off pitches until he received one that enabled him to place the ball where he wanted, reduced batting averages universally. Keeler's .313 was actually good for sixth place in the league, and behind it, New York's first American League team posted a winning record at 72-62.

Keeler adjusted to the new rules, and in 1904 he improved his numbers to 186 hits and a .343 batting average, each good for second place in the league. The Highlanders also improved, finishing in second place with a 92-59 record. However, the season was bittersweet. In the final game, a ninth inning wild pitch from New York pitcher Jack Chesbro handed both the game and the league pennant to the Boston Americans.

In 1905, the Highlanders finished in sixth place with a losing record, though Keeler finished second in the league in batting at .302 and fourth in hits with 169. But, in 1906 they were a successful team once again, finishing in second place by only three games with a 90-61 record. In what would turn out to be Keeler's last year as a full-time player, he finished second in the league with 96 runs scored while also ranking in tenth place with a .304 batting average and in fifth place with 180 hits.

In 1907, Keeler was 35 years old, and his batting average fell below .300 for the first time in his career, finishing at a mere .234. Correspondingly, in 107 games played, his total diminished to 50 runs scored, 7 stolen bases, and only 99 hits. As Keeler struggled, the Highlanders would also struggle, ultimately finishing in fifth place with a losing record. While Keeler would raise his batting average to .263 and .264 respectively over the next two seasons, he played in only 91 and 99 games, and he no longer ranked among the game's elite hitters. The Highlanders experienced lackluster records in those two seasons which led to several managerial changes. Keeler actually left the team with six weeks to go in the 1908 season because of disagreements with player-manager Norman Elberfeld. Though he stated that he was going to quit baseball, Keeler was later coaxed back and made the team's captain in 1909, the year that the team first adopted the NY logo that would become famous after they were rebranded the New York Yankees.

Following the 1909 season, the Highlanders released Keeler so that he could sign with the team of his choosing, and Keeler chose to reunite with former teammate John McGraw, then managing the New York Giants, to complete his major league career. During the season, Keeler, then age 38, served as a batting coach, an occasional pinch hitter, and even served as an umpire for one summer game. While his time on the field was limited, Keeler batted .300 in his final season, achieving three hits in ten at-bats.

Following his final major league game, Keeler spent the 1911 season with the Toronto Maple Leafs of the Eastern League, earning 43 hits in 39 games, and then he served as a coach or scout for several other teams in the years that followed. It is clear that, at that point in his life, Keeler was not driven by money, but rather by his love of the game. During his playing career, he had successfully invested in businesses and real estate so that he was able to live quite comfortably until the recession that followed the Great War. At that point, economic and health hardships caused him to sell his childhood home and to accept gifts from major league owners in order to cover his debts. His health continued to decline, confining him to bed in the winter of 1922. Keeler vowed to his visitors and well-wishers that he would live to see the New Year, and he did so, dying on New Year's Day 1923 from heart disease at the age of 50. As the *New York Times* noted in his obituary, "He was playing the game of life as he played the game of baseball – until the last man was out in the ninth." The lifelong bachelor left his entire $3500 estate to the woman who owned the house where he boarded.

More than a century after his final major league appearance, Keeler still holds the best career at-bat to strikeout ratio in major league history with a strikeout every 63.16 at-bats. Keeler's highest single-season strikeout total was 13, recorded in both 1902 and 1905, seasons when he had 559 and 560 at-bats respectively. In his 1899 season of 570 at-bats, he struck out only twice. He also ranked in the league's top ten in batting average for thirteen consecutive seasons. Keeler's speed was almost as great an asset as his bat control as 30 of his 33 career homeruns were inside-the-park, and he finished his career with 145 triples and 495 stolen bases. In short, Keeler was one of baseball's most dominant offensive players for almost two decades.

Keeler also made a positive impact upon those who played with him. On a fierce Baltimore team known for its readiness to brawl, Keeler was one of the more polite members who did not drink or swear. In the words of Jimmy Austin, an infielder who came into the major leagues as a teammate of Keeler's during Keeler's last full season, "Wee Willie Keeler was still a pretty good ballplayer, even then. He could loop 'em over the infield better than anybody I ever saw. Wonderful fellow. I was too shy to say anything to him, but he came to me one day and said, 'Jim, you've got a great career ahead of you. If I can help you in any way, you just say the word.' How about that?" A similar sentiment seems to have been shared by Keeler's opponents as Sam Crawford, in addition to praising Keeler's skill with a bat, noted that he was "A real nice little guy too, very friendly, always laughing and kidding."

One of the most famous and most admired ballplayers to carry baseball from the nineteenth to the twentieth century, Keeler was elected to the Hall of Fame in 1939, the final election year before the museum opened its doors for the first time.

Major League Debut: September 30, 1892, for the New York Giants

Final Major League Game: September 5, 1910, for the New York Giants

Career Batting Average: .341; NL Batting Champion 1897, 1898

Career Hits: 2,932; NL Leader 1897-98, 1900

Career Runs Batted In: 810

Career Stolen Bases: 495

Inducted to the Major League Baseball Hall of Fame: 1939

Keeler's Hall of Fame Plaque Reads:

WILLIE KEELER
"HIT'EM WHERE THEY AINT!"
BASEBALL'S GREATEST PLACE-HITTER;
BEST BUNTER. BIG LEAGUE CAREER
1892 TO 1919 WITH N.Y. GIANTS,
BALTIMORE ORIOLES, BROOKLYN SUPERBAS,
N.Y. HIGHLANDERS. NATIONAL LEAGUE
BATTING CHAMPION '97-'98.

MICHAEL JOSEPH "KING" KELLY

During the Civil War years, Washington DC experienced a period of activity and development unlike any other in the city's history. Washington began the War as a young, relatively small city, only seventy years old with only 61,122 residents as of 1860. In contrast, New Orleans (founded 1718) was home to 170,000, Philadelphia (founded 1682) housed over 500,000, and New York City (founded as a Dutch fur trading post in 1624) contained 1,175,000; each was a more seasoned and developed city than the nation's capital. During the War, change was everywhere. Population, construction, infrastructure, government and war planning were increasing exponentially. Mary Clemmer Ames, an author and Washington resident, offered this description: "Arid hill, and sodden plain showed alike the horrid trail of war. Forts bristled above every hill-top. Soldiers were entrenched at every gate-way. Shed hospitals covered acres on acres in every suburb. Churches, art-halls and private mansions were filled with the wounded and dying of the American armies. The endless roll of the army wagon seemed never still. The rattle of the anguish-laden ambulance, the piercing cries of the sufferers.... made morning, noon and night too dreadful to be borne." Hospitals did their best to respond to the 20,000 injured or wounded who flooded the city, and freed and runaway slaves congregated in large numbers, yet despite the disarray, President Lincoln could still, with some regularity, be spotted in the course of an unaccompanied ride on horseback.

In the midst of Washington's growth, tumult and proximity to the front, many Americans continued to live, work and raise their children. Such was the case for Catherine Kelly, who had moved to Washington with her children to endure the duration of her husband's service in the Union Army. Like so many, Mike and Catherine Kelly had come to the United States to escape the horror of the Potato Famine. Settling in Troy, NY, the couple had two boys, James and Mike (born New Year's Eve 1857), before Mike Kelly's

1862 enlistment, and eventually re-enlistment, for the Union. Catherine kept the family afloat, and James and Mike navigated an early childhood of school and frequent baseball games, surely enjoying the sights and wonder of the DC streets. Following Mike's return to his family, the Kellys moved to Patterson, NJ, where tragedy would finally reach them as Mike succumbed to illness, only to be followed by his wife, and James and Mike were left as orphans when the younger was just 13.

The loss of his parents meant that young Mike Kelly had to add jobs at silk and coal factories to his routine of school and baseball. His jobs required the completion of manual tasks rather than logging a regular number of hours, so the quicker Mike finished, the more time he was able to find for himself on the ball field. Also, with a friend named Jim McCormick, Mike expanded his interests to include amateur theatre. Still, Mike's primary love was baseball, and at the age of 15, he was recruited, along with McCormick, to Patterson's best team. Initially Mike was only a backup player, but within a couple of years, he would work his way into the position of starting catcher. For the next few years, Mike would play semi-pro ball in Patterson and other cities in the New York area. By 1877, McCormick persuaded the Columbus Buckeyes, with whom he was then playing, to sign Mike as his catcher. Mike did not immediately launch himself to stardom, batting only .156 that year, but when the Columbus team disbanded in September of that year, Mike had done enough to be offered a contract as a reserve player with the Cincinnati Red Stockings, who would later rename themselves the Cincinnati Reds in 1890 when they left the American Association to join the National League.

Mike began his major league career with the Red Stockings in May of 1878, and he did a serviceable job as a backup catcher and outfielder, but it was in 1879 that he began to distinguish himself. In that breakout season, Kelly was third in the league in batting average (.348), third in hits (120), fourth in runs scored (78), eighth in doubles (20), third in triples (12), fifth in homeruns (2) and tenth in runs batted in (47). In addition to his talent and offensive production, Kelly also became known for his baseball intelligence. Reportedly, in a game against Cap Anson's Chicago White Stockings, Kelly was called safe on a tag play at second base. As the Chicago players proceeded to argue the call with the umpire, Kelly realizing that he was not being defended, raced all the way home to score a run. In short, there seemed to be little that Kelly could do wrong in 1879, but he still faced his release by the Cincinnati club in September. The Red Stockings had lost upwards of $10,000 during the course of the season, and their owner determined that his only recourse was to release all of his players because he could not afford to issue their final pay checks.

Kelly's level of play had been impressive enough to earn him a place on a west coast barnstorming team following the 1879 season, a team that included Cap Anson, among other notable players. Anson, who was captain of Al Spalding's Chicago White Stockings, offered Kelly a place on the team, and after he held out briefly for salary negotiations, Kelly signed with the White Stockings as a free agent in December 1879. However, when he reported the following spring, Kelly's weight was heavier than Anson preferred, so Kelly became one of the first professional ballplayers to undergo a new enterprise of Anson's – spring training. The White Stockings then opened the season in Cincinnati, where Kelly had played the previous year, and Kelly won the game for Chicago by hitting a homerun, his only one of the season, in a 4-3 victory. Kelly quickly became popular with fans and fellow Chicago players alike, actually becoming more social than Anson would have liked as he moved into the lively and luxurious Palmer House Hotel, which hosted everyone from U.S. presidents to Oscar Wilde. It was at this time that Kelly took to drinking regularly, eventually leading to a clause in his contract that would reward good behavior. Still, Kelly finished the season tenth in the league in average (.291) and second in runs batted in (60) as the White Stockings easily finished in first place with a 67-17 record, a .798 winning percentage that is still a National League record, though the White Stockings would lose an inter-league playoff against the National Association's Washington Nationals.

King Kelly, 1887-1890
Old Judge (N172)
Courtesy of Library of Congress PPOC

Mike Kelly played with the Chicago White Stockings for the following six seasons, mostly as a catcher, but occasionally as an outfielder. During that period, Kelly established himself as a superstar, leading the league in doubles twice (1881-1882), batting average twice (1884 & 1886), and runs scored three times (1884-1886). He also posted a career-high 13 homeruns in 1884. In all, with Kelly, the White Stockings won five pennants, establishing themselves as the National League powerhouse of the era, though they did not experience similar success in inter-league championships. More broadly, baseball itself benefitted from Kelly's time in Chicago. It was during those years that he helped to establish the use of the glove, the mask, and the chest protector at the catching position. He is also credited with innovations such as the hit-and-run play, adjusting outfield positions, the infield shift, the double steal, and the hook slide. Kelly even provided the concept of the coaches' boxes as, while coaching third base in 1886, he ran out towards the shortstop position to provide a distraction to help his baserunner, a move that was not strictly illegal under the rules at that time. His good looks, strong play and exciting antics also brought fans of both genders and all ages to the ballpark. According to baseball historian Maclean Kennedy, author of *The Great Teams of Baseball*, who had the opportunity to see Kelly play, "There was never a better or more brilliant player. Colorful beyond description, he was the light and the life of the game... He was one of the quickest thinkers that ever took a signal. He originated more tricks than all players put together... As a drawing card, he was the greatest of his time." Ever the showman, Kelly was known to address the crowd between pitches, and he became the first American celebrity known to provide an autograph.

Of course, Kelly knew how popular and impactful he was, and, probably also driven by his excessive spending and profligate lifestyle, he frequently sought what he believed to be deserved increases in his salary, putting himself at odds with team ownership. One such period arose after the 1886 season, though Kelly was already being paid at or near the National League $2000 maximum salary. Kelly had posted exceptional numbers in 1886, but his drunkenness cost him a significant amount in team fines, about $250 of his $2000 salary. Excessive drinking on the team had been so bad that particular season that teammate Billy Sunday left abruptly in the summer because he could no longer weather the situation, stating "Goodbye. I'm going to Jesus Christ," and would from that point begin building his career as a famed evangelist. It was also true that, in losing their 1886 postseason series to the St. Louis Browns, the White Stockings did not get a share of the $15,000 gate receipts. Later, in his history of the game, Al Spalding would write that while everybody in Chicago liked Kelly, "Kelly's habits were not conducive to the best interests of the club or his team-mates. He was of a highly convivial nature, extremely fascinating and witty, and his example was demoralizing to discipline. Particularly was his influence objectionable upon the younger members of the nine." In short, Chicago owner Spalding decided that the benefits Kelly brought to his team were outweighed by the frustrations and that it would be more prudent to seek new talent, so he agreed to sell Kelly to the Boston Beaneaters for the previously unheard-of sum of $10,000. The Beaneaters then extended Kelly a $5,000 annual salary – the $2,000 league maximum and an additional $3,000 for the ability to use his photograph in their advertising.

If anything, Kelly's transition to Boston would be detrimental to him because he was able to further indulge in bad behavior. Boys gathered around him in the streets to seek an autograph, his image found its way onto the walls of Irish pubs throughout the city, and he was able to earn further income by endorsing products ranging from sleds to beverages to shoe polish. He continued to spend much of his money, and to leverage some of his fame, on drinking heavily. According to Anson, who had tried to keep an eye on Kelly while he played with Chicago, Kelly could, in just minutes, "consume enough whiskey to put an ordinary man under the table." He preferred whiskey to beer, but he was able to brag that he played baseball well enough that he would "never be broke." In accordance, his 1887 performance was excellent. He was tenth in the league with a .322 average, second with 34 doubles, and third with 84 stolen bases, a feat for which he was awarded a gold medal inscribed "champion base stealer" by the Boston Globe. The Beaneaters managed only a fifth-place finish with a 61-60 record, but their attendance was spectacular as tens of thousands of fans flooded each series to see Kelly play. Chicago's White Stockings, on the other hand, managed a third place 71-50 finish, but their attendance plummeted as fans boycotted the team from the season's open and only showed up in large numbers once Kelly returned to play against Anson's club.

Following the 1887 season, Kelly barnstormed in the west and then returned to theater with a Boston production entitled *Rag Baby*, and during the opening show he reportedly received a full minute's standing ovation after saying his first line. Work also began on *Play Ball: Stories of the Ballfield*, a ghost-written series of autobiographical stories that would be published in 1888, making it the first autobiography of a baseball player.

Michael J. "King" Kelly, *America's National Game*, pg. 294

Throughout 1888 and 1889, Kelly's performance remained consistently stellar. Both in Boston and beyond, he was becoming known as "King" Kelly or "The Only", names applied to him by the media. The Beaneaters continued to invest in their club, and with King Kelly as their foundation, they found a path to improvement, finishing in second place with an 83-45 record in 1889, only one game shy of the New York Giants. It was the first time in major league history that the pennant was decided on the season's final day.

Throughout it all, Kelly remained as popular as ever. Beyond his offensive numbers, he provided fans an individual focal point during games. Kelly was known as someone who would readily take advantage of the single umpire that manned games during much of his career. When the umpire's attention was elsewhere, Kelly would cut bases, sometimes even cutting across the middle of the field. He was known for carrying an extra baseball in his pocket in case he could substitute one to his advantage while playing the outfield. One story of his outfield play, as a game progressed into extra innings, involves a deep drive being hit by the opposing team. Kelly leapt and caught the ball, and he immediately ran towards the clubhouse as the umpire called the ballgame because of darkness. Kelly's teammates reached the clubhouse to find him sitting with his hands empty, admitting freely, "It was a mile over my head." As a catcher, he would drop his mask in such a way as would create an obstacle for a runner attempting to slide across home plate. Mike Kelly was a showman who packaged excitement and cunning with first-rate ability, and as a result he found himself a celebrity. This sometimes had negative results, as when Kelly was fined $100 by the Beaneaters' manager for not reporting to the field as required, and it was widely known and written that he could be careless and indifferent on the field on some days. But on the other days, he was sensational, and he continued to receive adulation from the public at large. In 1889, a song entitled "Slide, Kelly, Slide", based on the chant Boston fans often used when Kelly cut across the bases, became an immediate hit, selling one million copies of sheet music, and the song went on to become America's first hit record in 1892, when recording technology allowed for it's recording to be sold commercially.

In fact, as the 1890 season approached, Mike Kelly's value, and his ability to capitalize upon it, provided the basis of motivation for major league players, who were frustrated with their capped salaries as interest and attendance grew, to attempt forming and marketing their own major league: the Players' League. In the era of the Homestead Strike and the Pullman Strike, when the American Federation of Labor grew due to dissatisfaction with the Knights of Labor, American labor actively pursued organization as a means towards better wages and working conditions. The same was largely true in baseball, where the Brotherhood of Professional Base-Ball Players had served as the sport's first union since the mid-1880s. After failing to satisfactorily elicit concessions from management regarding the reserve clause and salary limitations, the Brotherhood, with backing from the American Federation of Labor, promoted a new major league organized by the players themselves with a focus on parity. Like many of baseball's stars, Kelly left his National League club to become part of the Players' League as a player-manager for the Boston Reds. "I'm one of the bosses now," Kelly purported said. He played well, and he led the team to a first-place finish with a record of 81-48, but the business side of baseball management frustrated him, though he stayed loyal to the players' cause.

One of the era's great stories involves a mid-summer Boston Reds trip to Chicago to play the Players' League Pirates, managed by Charles Comisky. During his stay in Chicago, Kelly met with Al Spalding, still the owner of the National League Chicago franchise, which was then known as the Colts and still led by Cap Anson. During the meeting, Spalding offered Kelly a $10,000 check and a three-year contract at any amount Kelly cared to name. Kelly asked for time to think about the offer and took a walk before returning with his answer, which was no. When Spalding asked in astonishment why Kelly didn't want the $10,000, Kelly responded that he did indeed want it, but that he couldn't go back on the other players. He then proceeded to borrow $500 from Spalding in order to make ends meet.

King Kelly, 1888
Goodwin Champions (N162)
Courtesy of Library of Congress PPOC

Of course, Kelly's loyal fans prevented him from meeting financial ruin. While the Players' League was a problematic business venture, he found stability in his Boston circle as friends contributed to buy Kelly a $10,000 house and a horse and carriage as gifts in 1890. The house would not remain in Kelly's hands long, instead being put up for sale in 1893 for $123 in back taxes. Similarly, the Players' League venture was short-lived, with 1890 being its only effective season due to inadequate financial backing despite relatively good attendance. As the League ended, Kelly's Boston Reds team was moved into the American Association, which was one of the League's lasting impacts, in addition to beginning the practice of employing two umpires a game, which countered base cutting and other such tricks used by players such as Kelly in the past. With limited offers due to his continued drinking and an increasing weight problem, Kelly ended up signing with the American Association Cincinnati Reds for just $1750, and the team was renamed Kelly's Killers in an effort to market based on the move, with Kelly installed as player-manager.

Kelly's Killers failed as an experiment in Cincinnati due to poor players, inadequate financial backing and poor attendance, and the club did not survive the season. Instead, with a 43-57 in early August, Kelly's Killers was dissolved and moved to Milwaukee, as the Brewers, to finish the 1891 season. The Brewers finished with a record of 21-15, without the presence of Mike Kelly, but dissolved when the American Association dissolved at the end of the 1891 season.

Instead of moving to Milwaukee when Kelly's Killers met its demise, Mike Kelly accepted an offer to return to the Boston Reds of the American Association, and he played four games with them, earning four hits in fifteen plate appearances, before jumping leagues to accept a better offer with the National League Boston Beaneaters. Kelly didn't play much for the Beaneaters after his arrival, only sixteen games, but the team went on an eighteen-game winning streak immediately after his arrival, propelling them to a first-place finish. Interestingly, the Boston Reds also won a pennant in 1891 in the American Association. Considering that the Boston Reds of the Players' League had won their pennant the year before, Boston baseball teams won pennants in three different major leagues over the course of two seasons, and Mike Kelly was unique in that he had played on all three pennant-winning ballclubs.

Another important portion of the Kelly legend was built during some point of the 1890 or 1891 season. Legend has it that Kelly was on the bench for his team when Ed Delahanty, one of baseball's greatest hitters of the era, came to bat with two outs and the bases loaded. Delahanty proceeded to pop the ball into the air in front of the Boston dugout, and Kelly jumped up and yelled, "Kelly now catching for Boston," inserting himself into the game in mid-play, and he caught the ball. While research has suggested that the home plate umpire did not allow the out, thereby nullifying the trick, Kelly's effort did prompt a major league rule requirement that substitutions be announced to umpires before a pitch is thrown.

Kelly would win another pennant with the Boston Beaneaters in 1892, but he struggled throughout the season. He only managed to play in 78 games and batted a feeble .189. The Beaneaters continued on to defeat the Cleveland Spiders five games to none in the post-season championships, but again Kelly did not substantially contribute, earning no hits in eight at-bats. Following his release from Boston, Kelly signed to play with the New York Giants in 1893, but he played only twenty games, batting .269 with a double as his only extra-base hit, before his major league career came to an end.

Kelly played some minor league ball with the Allentown team of the Pennsylvania State League in 1894, moving with the team to finish the season in Yonkers, New York. Kelly and his wife, Agnes, apparently had their only child in late 1893 or 1894, and there was continued pressure for Mike to provide a satisfactory income. As a result, he continued to work in vaudeville, where he had appeared steadily since the mid-1880s, billed as "King Kelly, the Monarch of the Baseball Field." He often performed comedies, but he was also well-known for his recitations of "Casey at the Bat" and sometimes would deliver skits or be cast into plays. In the fall of 1894, Kelly performed in a piece entitled "O'Dowd's Neighbors" for a number of dates in New York before returning to Boston for dates at the Palace Theater. The advertisement in the Boston papers read "Slide, Kelly, Slide. Palace Theater. The London Gaiety Girls, Chaperoned by King Kelly, the Famous $10,000 Base Ballist." However, Kelly caught a cold in New York, and it developed into pneumonia by the time he reached Boston. He was rushed to a private hospital room, but on November 8, 1894, baseball's most celebrated player died at the age of 36 before any family member could reach his side. While circumstances are unclear, it seems that Mike Kelly's child also died in 1894, and unfortunately Kelly had no living family members to represent him when he was inducted into the Major League Baseball Hall of Fame in 1945.

In addition to being one of the most skilled baseball players of his era, Kelly was certainly the most dynamic. He brought celebrity to the sport and to America as a whole. Kelly also provided great nuanced innovation to baseball, doing perhaps as much as anyone to help it develop from amateur pastime to professional sport.

Professional Debut: May 01, 1878, for the Cincinnati Reds

Final Major League Game: September 02, 1893, for the New York Giants

Career Batting Average: .308

2-time NL Batting Champion: .354 in 1884 and .388 in 1886

Career Stolen Bases: 368

Career Runs Scored: 1,357; led league 1884-1886

6-time National League Champion (1880-1882, 1885-1886, 1892);

> Players' League Champion (1890)

Inducted to the Major League Baseball Hall of Fame: 1945

Kelly's Hall of Fame Plaque Reads:

> MIKE J. (KING) KELLY
> COLORFUL PLAYER AND AUDACIOUS
> BASE-RUNNER. IN 1887 FOR BOSTON
> HE HIT .394 AND STOLE 84 BASES.
> HIS SALE FOR $10,000 WAS ONE OF
> THE BIGGEST DEALS OF BASEBALL'S
> EARLY HISTORY.

CHARLES AUGUSTUS "KID" NICHOLS

In early June 1949, more than 40 years removed from his playing career, Charles Nichols received a letter from Ty Cobb, the baseball legend who had received 98.2% of the induction vote for the Baseball Hall of Fame's inaugural class, a record that would stand until Tom Seaver's 1992 election. The letter read, in part, "I have an announcement from the National Baseball Hall of Fame, that you have been elected as a member. This gives me great pleasure because I knew quite well from your record that you belonged in the Baseball Hall of Fame. I have been much interested as a fellow ball player, admiring what you established with your ability. You might not have known of my interest and to be sure, I am writing you this to say that it pleases me greatly that you have been elected." While Cobb's career had barely overlapped with Nichols', the Georgia Peach was an adamant proponent of Nichol's greatness. In 1948, Cobb is said to have told a reporter, "You're a bit too young to remember, but I knew a pitcher who was a real pitcher. His name was Kid Nichols. He was with the Boston Nationals early in the century." Cobb then drew from his pocket a notes sheet regarding Nichols' career statistics that he regularly carried and used it to extol the greatness of one of baseball's early careers. While Cobb was not Nichols' only supporter for Hall of Fame induction, he was perhaps the most influential, and his incredible baseball intelligence made his endorsement one that could not be discounted.

Baseball intelligence was a characteristic that Nichols' surely understood. After all, Cy Young said of Kid Nichols, "Kid Nichols forgot more baseball than 90% of us will ever know." Young, the career leader in pitching victories with 511, 150 more than Nichols' 361 total which ranks him in seventh place all-time, debuted in the same year as Nichols, and he openly admitted that Nichols was the better pitcher for the first decade of their careers. In fact, Nichols' career legacy was built almost entirely upon

105

his first ten seasons, and it can be said to have been built upon a single pitch: a fastball that was not as remarkable as those of contemporaries Young and Amos Rusie. Still, Nichols began his career with consistent greatness that has not since been repeated by any other major league pitcher.

Charles Nichols was born in Madison, Wisconsin, on September 14, 1869, fifty-five years to the day from the evening that Francis Scott Key wrote the words that would become the lyrics to the *Star-Spangled Banner* after witnessing the Battle of Baltimore. His father, Robert, a butcher, had several children from each of two marriages, and the large family provided Charles with no shortage of baseball competition. Two of his siblings, James and John, played in the National Association of Base Ball before Charles' birth, and he would grow up playing with siblings Will and George. The family moved to Kansas City sometime near Charles' twelfth birthday, and by the time he was sixteen, he had earned positions on amateur teams. Charles played well enough to be asked to join the professional Kansas City Cowboys of the Western League in 1887.

In his first professional game, June 14, 1887, Nichols was the winning pitcher against Lincoln, Nebraska. At that point, he had already been given the nickname "Kid" because of his size (about 135 pounds) and his youthful appearance. He won 18 games for the season, but he was not re-signed. Instead, in 1878, Kid split his time between two ballclubs. He built a record of 11-8 with the Memphis Grays of the Southern League before the league disbanded in June, and then he returned home to pitch for Kansas City's Blues, finishing in the Western Association with a 16-2 record and a league-leading 1.14 earned run average. His 1889 Western Association season for the Omaha Omahogs brought him to the attention of Major League teams, as he finished with a record of 39-8.

Kid Nichols signed with the National League Boston Beaneaters in September 1889, and then he married Jennie Curtin before moving east to join the team for 1890. Kid Nichols made his debut against Brooklyn on April 23. His rookie season was a success as he led the league with 7 shutouts and finished sixth in the league in victories with a 27-19 record, third place with 222 strikeouts, and second place with a 2.23 earned run average. He also completed all 47 games that he started, and he served as a finisher in one other. The season's clear highlight was a May 12 contest where twenty-year-old Kid Nichols faced off in a duel against nineteen-year-old Amos Rusie of the New York Giants. Both pitchers threw shutout baseball through the first nine innings, and the game remained scoreless in the top of the thirteenth inning as Nichols struck out Rusie to begin the frame. The next batter, legendary 1890s slugger Mike Tiernan then hit a tremendous homerun to centerfield (actually landing in nearby Brotherhood Park where a Players' League game was being played at the same time) before Nichols retired the side. As the home team, the New York Giants had elected to bat first, in order to have an opportunity at the ball while it was still lively, so Rusie had to retire the Beaneaters in the bottom of the 13th to complete the game. Nichols suffered the loss, but he had distinguished himself in one of the most talked-about and admired baseball games of the era.

In 1891, as star players returned to the National League from the failed Players' League, Nichols improved to a 30-17 record with a 2.39 earned run average and 240 strikeouts (each placing him in the league's top four). The Beaneaters won the pennant, finishing three and a half games ahead of Anson's Colts. The next two seasons delivered two more pennants as Nichols' pitching continued to dominate. He posted a 35-16 record with 192 strikeouts and a 2.84 earned run average in 1892, and when the pitching

Kid Nichols, 1887-1890
Old Judge (N172)
Courtesy of Library of Congress PPOC

mound was moved from 50 feet to 60 feet, 6 inches, from home plate in 1893, he went 34-14 while completing 43 of his 44 games started, though his strikeouts understandably dropped to 94 and his earned run average rose to 3.52. In the one postseason series that the Beaneaters played, Nichols completed two games of Boston's 5-0-1 1892 World Championship Series win against the Cleveland Spiders, allowing only two runs in the process.

Boston finished in third place during the 1894 campaign, but Nichols provided another sensational season, finishing with a 32-13 record. The next two seasons saw the team fall even farther in the league's rankings, as they finished in fifth place and fourth place respectively, despite Nichols' records of 27-16 and 30-14. In the seasons since Boston's three consecutive pennants, the Baltimore Orioles had won three of their own.

1897 provided a season of competition between Boston and Baltimore that found the two teams fighting down to the wire. Nichols led the league in victories with a 31-11 record, and he also led the league with three saves and 368 total innings pitched. However, on September 21, Boston lost to Baltimore 22-5 with Nichols surrendering twelve runs in the first inning. Three days later, Boston began a three-game series in Baltimore with only six games remaining in the season. Nichols won the first and third games of the series, with Baltimore winning the middle game, and Boston managed to finish the season in first place, just two games ahead of the Orioles. While Baltimore won the post-season Temple Cup series against Boston four games to one, Nichols and the Beaneaters had won the longer fight of the season.

In 1898, Nichols again led the league in victories while posting a 31-12 record. He also led the league with 50 pitching appearances and four saves as he completed 40 of his 42 starts and finished 8 other contests. His 2.13 earned run average was the best of his career. The rest of Boston's team followed Nichols' lead, earning another National League pennant, this time finishing six full games ahead of second-place Baltimore. The pennant was Boston's last of the decade, just as the season had provided the final 30-win season of Nichols' career, a mark that he had achieved 7 times in his first 9 seasons.

Over the next three seasons, as the century changed, Kid Nichols finished with win-loss records of 21-19, 13-16, and 19-16 that, at first glance, suggest a significant drop-off from his star performances of earlier years. However, while he was injured during part of the 1900 season, he remained otherwise quite durable during those seasons, finishing 37 of 37 starts, 25 of 27 and 33 of 34 respectively. He also threw four shutouts each season, ranking him at or among the league leaders, and he finished with respectable earned run averages of 2.99, 3.07 and 3.22. During those years,

Nichols also accepted postseason opportunities to coach collegiate baseball at Amherst, Yale and Brown.

Kid Nichols, 1895
Mayo's Cut Plug (N300)
Courtesy of Library of Congress PPOC

In 1902, Nichols left the Major Leagues at age 32 in order to manage and pitch for the Western League's Kansas City Blue Stockings, in which he had bought an interest. His team won the pennant in 1902 as Nichols went 27-7 with a 1.82 earned run average, and they posted another winning season in 1903 as he went 21-12 with an earned run average of 2.51. However, the Western League was forced to restructure before the 1903 season concluded, and in the midst of a shuffling that placed the Kansas City team in the American Association, Kid Nichols decided to instead return to the major leagues by accepting a 1904 managing job with the St. Louis Cardinals.

The Cardinals finished the 1904 season under Nichols with a 75-79 record, a significant improvement from their 43-94 finish a season earlier. Nichols had also proved effective on the mound, finishing with a personal record of 21-13 with a 2.02 earned run average. The following year saw Nichols relieved of his managerial duties after a 5-9 team record to start the season. Some suggest that the slow start was met with such a swift response because Nichols clashed with Stanley Robison who, at that point, was asserting more control as co-owner. Nichols was unconditionally released later in the season as he had managed to post only a 1-5 pitching record while allowing a career-high 5.40 earned run average. Once released by St. Louis, Nichols was quickly claimed by former teammate Hugh Duffy, who was managing the Philadelphia Phillies. The Phillies finished in fourth place, but in his time with them, Nichols posted a 10-6 record with a 2.27 earned run average, clearly benefitting from the transition to a new team.

Nichols returned to the Phillies in 1906 for his age 36 season, but he began to suffer debilitating pain in his sides that would later be diagnosed as pleuritis. He managed only 11 innings pitched, including 1 strikeout and 13 walks, before he retired on May 18 with an 0-1 record an 9.82 earned run average for the season.

Over the next 30 years, Nichols remained active in baseball. He scouted, managed at the collegiate and minor league levels, and he played on semi-pro team and in old-timers' games. Nichols also patented an electronic scoreboard, operated a series of bowling alleys, won the Kansas City bowling championship, and operated a movie and vaudeville house with former major leaguer Joe Tinker. He also became a grandfather and a great-grandfather.

1895 Boston Beaneaters

Nichols is quoted as having said, "We played for the love of the game; there were few holdouts. We wanted to pitch every day; to win more games than the other guy – not for the money, but for the glory of winning." Nichols posted 298 victories in his first ten seasons and 362 overall in a career that was cut short by injury. He is baseball's youngest pitcher to win 300 games, accomplishing that feat at age 30. His career victories, which ranked third at the time of his retirement, now place him seventh all-time, though more than 110 additional seasons have passed. In 1949, Nichols was finally inducted to baseball's Hall of Fame, along with Mordecai Brown, who as a rising star had been the second-best pitcher (with 1 more win but 7 more losses than Nichols while posting a 2.22 era compared to Nichols' 1.82) in the Western League during Nichols' 1902 season with Kansas City.

Kid Nichols is said to have been proud of two things above all others: his Hall of Fame induction and the fact that he was never removed from a game in favor of a reliever. The latter assertion is, in fact, untrue. Nichols started 562 games during the course of his major league pitching career; he completed 532, a 94.66% completion rate. Such a truth is perhaps even more impressive than the alleged perfect completion rate. It demonstrates that Nichols could have been, and sometimes was, replaced. There was no pressure to keep him in a game merely because of his reputation or lingering statistical perfection. Nichols earned each of his innings, and in 532 of his 562 career starts, he was his team's best option to finish the contest. The statistical greatness of his first ten years has stood the test of time, and it is corroborated by the testimony of Cy Young and Ty Cobb, two of his contemporaries who surely knew greatness when they saw it. More than a century after his playing career ended, Kid Nichols retains a position among the game's all-time greats.

Major League Debut: April 23, 1890, for the Boston Beaneaters

Final Major League Game: May 18, 1906, for the Philadelphia Phillies

Win-Loss Record: 361-208

National League Wins Leader: 1896-1898

Career Earned Run Average: 2.95

Career Strikeouts: 1,873

Inducted to the Major League Baseball Hall of Fame: 1949

Nichols' Hall of Fame Plaque Reads:

> CHARLES A. (KID) NICHOLS
> RIGHT HANDED PITCHER WHO WON 30 OR
> MORE GAMES FOR SEVEN CONSECUTIVE
> YEARS (1891-97) AND WON AT LEAST 20
> GAMES FOR TEN CONSECUTIVE SEASONS
> (1890-99) WITH BOSTON N.L. ALSO PITCHED
> FOR ST. LOUIS AND PHILADELPHIA N.L. ONE
> OF FEW PITCHERS TO WIN MORE THAN 300
> GAMES, HIS MAJOR LEAGUE RECORD BEING
> 360 VICTORIES, 202 DEFEATS.

JAMES HENRY "ORATOR JIM" O'ROURKE

The National League was founded on February 26, 1876, as a replacement for the National Association of Professional Baseball Players, which lacked strong centralized authority. The creation of Chicago White Stockings owner William A. Hulbert, the league began with eight charter teams. The National League's first game was scheduled for April 22, 1876, a contest between the Philadelphia Athletics and the Boston Red Stockings at Philadelphia's Jefferson Street Grounds, 100 years after the United States had been born in that same city. A crowd of about 3,000 fans gathered for that first game with no possible way of anticipating the new league's success and longevity. As a part of the history witnessed that day, Boston's twenty-five-year-old Jim O'Rourke stepped to the plate in the first inning and delivered the first base hit in National League history – a sharp single to left field. Ironically, O'Rourke had almost not played in the game at all as he had been sitting out in protest of the salary that had been offered him. Wisely, Boston's ownership gave in to O'Rourke's $1600 salary demand, which doubled his salary of the previous season, in time to place him with the team for the league's opening game. In addition to his momentous first hit, O'Rourke would go on to deliver one of nineteenth century baseball's most storied and acclaimed careers.

Born in 1850 in East Bridgeport, Connecticut, Jim O'Rourke was a middle child, the second of two sons. The children were first-generation Americans, the product of a loving Irish couple who had settled into farming. As a result, much of Jim's early life was split between school and farm work, but he and his brother John latched onto baseball as a pastime, playing from an early age. Jim, a year younger than his brother, established himself as a right-handed outfielder for local recreational teams such as the Bridgeport Ironsides and the Unions by the time he was a teenager. By the time he was seventeen, Jim had built his skills to a level that earned him a position as a substitute outfielder with the Stratford Osceolas, a regional semi-pro team.

Unfortunately, during the winter of 1868, Jim's baseball rise was subverted by the realities of life when his father, Henry, died of tetanus, leaving Jim and his brother John to help their widowed mother with her grief and the family farm. As he balanced his new responsibilities, Jim returned to play with the local Union recreational team the following year. 1870 found him with slightly more availability, and he returned to the semi-pro Stratford team, located slightly less than three miles from the family farm, as a regular outfielder and backup catcher. The 1870 season was largely a successful one, but the Osceolas were swept for the state championship by the rival Middletown Mansfields. Still, Jim had found a suitable balance of sport and responsibility, and he returned the following season to lead Stratford in taking the championship from the Mansfields. As they licked their wounds from their loss, the Middletown Mansfields accepted an opportunity to enter the professional National Association, and they sought to improve their lineup by signing Jim O'Rourke and pitcher Frank Buttery from the Osceolas, by whose hands they had suffered.

A professional contract was a fantastic opportunity for O'Rourke, but a transition to Mansfield, located almost forty-five miles from the family farm, was simply not a practical possibility. To get their man, the Mansfields had to concede to an unusual demand from Jim's mother: they had to find someone to assume his responsibilities on the family farm while he was away for the playing season. Once that was done, Jim was free to pursue his opportunity, and after marrying Anna Kehoe, a recent immigrant from Ireland, he moved to Mansfield to begin his new career. Signed as a catcher, Jim actually spent almost twice as much time at shortstop, with other brief stints at third and first base. While Jim's fielding was not a strength during his rookie season, his offense was solid as he finished with a .273 batting average and more hits than games played. Overshadowing O'Rourke's individual achievements were the realities of the Mansfields, who found that they could not compete with the larger market teams of Baltimore, Boston and New York. In a move that exemplified the fragility of the National Association, the Middletown team decided to end its season and its affiliation with the NA on August 14th, thereby returning Jim to work on the family farm after having only played twenty-three professional games.

Nonetheless, Jim had made an impression on the National Association's other teams, and he was offered a contract by the Boston Red Stockings. Following his Mansfields experience, and with his wife pregnant with their first child, Jim sought and received written guarantee of his salary for the full season before signing. The move proved to be a positive one as O'Rourke's fielding improved respectably and his offense improved dramatically. As the team won the pennant with a 43-16 record, Jim ranked eighth in the league with a .350 batting average, sixth with 79 runs scored and tenth with 49 runs batted in. He was also in the league's top ten in hits (sixth with 98), doubles (second with 21), stolen bases (sixth with 9), slugging percentage (eighth at .450) and total bases (fifth with 126). Still, Jim's most defining moment may have actually occurred before playing a single game that season. Manager Harry Wright, in anticipating the Boston fan reaction to O'Rouke's Irish heritage, recommended a name change to a more English moniker such as Rourke. O'Rourke refused, reportedly proclaiming, "I would rather die than give up my father's name." Also, on the advice of his mother, Jim began to use a portion of his salary to further his education in order to secure a life after baseball.

After an offseason spent at the family farm and in study, Jim's 1874 season confirmed his star status. Though his batting average dropped to .314, his overall production increased as he finished in the league's top ten in hits (fifth with 104), doubles (sixth with 15), triples (fourth with 8), homeruns (first with 5), total bases (second with 150), stolen bases (second with 11), runs (second with 82) and runs batted in (second with 61). Reaping the benefits, the Red Stockings repeated as champions of the National Association with an improved 52-18 record. For most of the team, the season's highlight must have been a mid-season exhibition tour of Great Britain. By all accounts, the tour, which included Jim's victory in a distance throwing contest, was successful in terms of goodwill but not so in relation to financial reward. In an attempt to recoup some of its financial losses, the Boston team assessed each player $100 for travel costs after the trip was done. Though at the time he could not find a way to avoid making payment, O'Rourke resented the power that his team had over him, and he vowed to stand up to it when necessary in the future.

Another offseason of farm work and study led Jim O'Rourke in the 1875 season, which saw similar success. Once again, he ranked in the league's top ten in several offensive categories: homeruns (first with 6), total bases (ninth with 151), triples (sixth with 7), stolen bases (eighth with 17), runs (third with 97) and runs batted in (third with 72). Correspondingly, Boston once again won the National Association pennant, this time with a record of 71-8. It was the club's fourth consecutive National Association pennant in the league's five-year history, and it would be the NA's final pennant as the league dissolved, in part because of Boston's dominance, which was contrasted by the instability and inability to compete demonstrated by other NA franchises. Next came the creation of the National League, with the Boston team continuing its existence as a founding franchise. While most of the 1875 Red Stockings team capitalized on the team's success and the chaos of the dissolving National Association to leave for more lucrative contracts offered by the Chicago White Stockings, O'Rourke decided to remain in New England, but he would not concede to anything less than a doubling of his salary in the weeks ahead of the National League's first game.

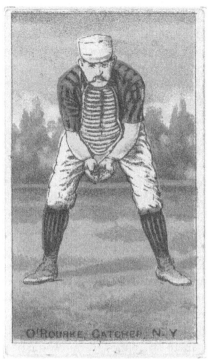

Jim O'Rourke, 1887
Buchner Gold Coin (N284)
Courtesy of Library of Congress PPOC

Following the National League's first hit, O'Rourke would go on to collect more than 2,100 hits in his National League career. Over the course of the next seventeen seasons, he would rank second in the major leagues in games played, at-bats, hits, doubles, total bases, and runs scored, a testament to his consistency and longevity.

In the early years of the National League, O'Rourke found himself a member of the Boston Red Caps, a new team name developed to avoid confusion with the Red Stockings team of Cincinnati. Having lost many of his stronger teammates, Jim still had individual success, ranking again in the top ten for batting average (ninth at .327), doubles (seventh with 17), homeruns (third with 2), total bases (eighth with 131), and runs (tenth with 61), but the Red Caps finished only in fourth place with a 39-31 record as they adjusted to the reality of a much more competitive league.

In 1877, O'Rourke combined a career high .362 batting average with league leading statistics in walks (20), on-base percentage (.407) and runs (68). The result, when combined with new Red Caps ownership and more experienced teammates, was Boston's first National League championship with a much-improved 42-18 record. Despite the team's success, O'Rourke found himself in conflict with new team owner Arthur Soden as Jim refused to pay a league fee of $30 for his uniform and a team fee of $20 for laundering. While 1878 saw Boston repeat its team success with a first-place 41-19 record, O'Rourke's individual production dropped significantly. The combination of his offensive struggles with his struggles with team ownership led Jim to join teammate George Wright in leaving Boston for the Providence Grays ballclub in 1879 as he sought to revitalize his career.

Jim O'Rourke, 1887-1890
Old Judge (N172)
Courtesy of Library of Congress PPOC

In short, Jim O'Rourke's move to the Providence Grays proved to be a tremendous success. He led the league with a .371 on-base percentage while finishing second in hits (126) and batting average (.348). The Grays, in only their second National League season, won the league pennant with a 59-25 record, finishing five full games ahead of the league's second place finisher, the Boston Red Caps.

Having proven his value, Jim returned to the Boston Red Caps for the 1880 season, in no small part because it provided him the opportunity to play in the same outfield as his brother John, who had joined the team during the previous season. The season was one of trade-offs as Jim saw his average drop to .275, but he led the league in homeruns for the third and final time of his career. Further, while he was able to play alongside his brother for the season, the season was not a successful one. Boston fell even further in the standings, finishing in sixth place with a losing 40-44 record. At season's end, when neither O'Rourke brother was reserved by Boston for the 1881 season, John decided to retire from baseball at the age of 32 to accept a more stable job with the New Haven railroad, and Jim accepted an opportunity as player/manager for the Buffalo Bisons.

Managing in Buffalo appears to have agreed with O'Rourke. His own performance was solid, though not stellar, as he returned to a .302 batting average with 71 runs scored but hit no homeruns. However, he was teamed with other future Hall of Famers in Pud Galvin, Deacon White and Dan Brouthers, and the team won more games than they lost, finishing in third place with a 45-38 record. Jim must have also found some satisfaction in the fact that his team finished seven full games in front of the sixth place Boston Red Caps. 1881 also provided one of the strongest examples of the eloquence that resulted in "Orator" Jim's nickname when his shortstop, Johnny Peters, asked for a $10 salary advance. O'Rourke's reported reply was, "The exigencies of the occasion and the condition of our exchequer will not permit anything of that sort at this period of our existence. Subsequent developments in the field of finance may remove the present gloom and we may emerge into a condition where we may see our way clear to reply in the affirmative to your exceedingly modest request." His dedication to his education was clearly emerging, and though he did not share in the drinking and smoking habits of his sometimes rabble-rousing team, O'Rourke led them effectively.

The next two seasons followed suit as O'Rourke posted consistent personal numbers and his team finished in fourth and fifth place respectively, each time with a winning record. Unfortunately, Jim's personal life was not as fortunate – he lost his second daughter, Anna, to a sudden illness in September 1883. Having always prevented a reserve clause from being incorporated into his Buffalo contract, O'Rourke notified the team in advance that the 1884 season would be his last with them as he felt the need to be closer to his family during the playing season. 1884 then saw a resurgence in Jim's performance. He led the league with 162 hits and a .347 batting average while also delivering 33 doubles, 5 homeruns, 63 runs batted in and a career-high 119 runs scored. Further, the team's play was excellent, and though they finished in third place, they posted a 64-47 record.

O'Rourke's success brought him an abundance of opportunities as the 1885 season approached, and he signed a well-negotiated deal with the New York Giants. Not only was he able to join a team full of future Hall of Famers such as Buck Ewing, Tim Keefe, Mickey Welch, Roger Connor and John Montgomery Ward, but Jim was also able to negotiate a $4000 contract without managerial responsibilities or a reserve clause. He was free to spend Sundays with his family in East Bridgeport, and with some influence from Ward, he was able to get the Giants to underwrite his tuition and expenses as he enrolled at Yale University Law School. Studies, however, were to wait until the offseason. In the meantime, O'Rourke performed in accordance with his reputation, delivering a .300 batting average, 21 doubles, 5 homeruns, a league-leading 16 triples and 119 runs scored. The Giants also found tremendous success, posting a 85-27 record, but they fell two games short of the league championship, which was won by Cap Anson's Chicago White Stockings.

Jim O'Rourke, 1888-1889
Old Judge (N173)
Courtesy of Library of Congress PPOC

Following the season's end, O'Rourke began his studies at Yale Law School, and at the same time he found that he may soon face trouble with baseball's contractual provisions as the National League implemented a $2000 players' salary cap. Luckily O'Rourke didn't face any immediate consequences, as the New York Giants' owner didn't agree with the concept of the salary cap and quickly resigned him to a $3000 contract without a reserve clause for 1886. Still, O'Rourke and teammates John Montgomery

Ward and Tim Keefe recognized the importance of labor unity in baseball and founded the Brotherhood of Professional Base Ball Players. During the season, O'Rourke continued his steady play, but the Giants slipped to third place and then to fourth over the next two seasons.

In the months following the 1887 season, O'Rourke completed his studies at Yale with a Bachelor's in Law and Legislation, and he promptly passed the bar examination and was admitted to the practice of law. On the baseball field, O'Rourke's performance began to slip, but the New York Giants won the 1888 pennant by nine games before moving forward to defeat the American Association St. Louis Browns six games to four for the 1888 World Championship. After working to establish his law practice in the offseason, O'Rourke returned to New York rejuvenated, and he proceed to post a .321 batting average with 89 runs scored and 81 runs batted in. The Giants once again won the National League pennant, though by only a game. They then defeated the American Association Brooklyn Bridegrooms six games to three in the 1889 World Series, the series that provided the foundation for the Giants/Dodgers rivalry of years to come. Jim was particularly effective in that World Series, batting .389 with 2 doubles, 2 triples, 2 homeruns, 7 runs scored and 7 runs batted in during his 36 at-bats.

Unfortunately, the success found by O'Rourke and the Giants could not overcome the tensions developing between the National League and its players. Since the attempted $2000 salary cap implementation in 1885, the League had made increasing attempts to control and limit players' salaries. It had also become apparent that the League would not negotiate in good faith with the Brotherhood. As a result, Ward, O'Rourke and the rest of the Brotherhood broke from the National League to form the Players' League, a player-controlled league that drew most of the star talent from both the National League and the American Association. Due to a lack of financial backing, the Players' League lasted only a single season before its players were forced to return to their previous teams with their salary caps and reserve clauses. During that 1890 season, however, O'Rourke performed well, even considering the dilution of talent that came with the development of a third professional league. He batted .360 for the season with career highs in doubles (37), homeruns (9) and runs batted in (115). In addition, his Players' League New York Giants opened Brotherhood Park, a facility that would become known as the Polo Grounds.

O'Rourke returned to the National League New York Giants as an outfield and partial shareholder for the next two seasons. He played well at the age of forty, batting .295 with 5 homeruns, 92 runs and 95 runs batted in during the 1891 season in which the Giants finished in third place. He returned in 1892 to bat .304, but his season was shortened after a confrontation with manager Patrick Powers. As the Giants descended to eighth place, Powers decided to release many of his aging star players, a move that was supported by primary owner John Day. O'Rourke confronted Powers upon finding out that he would be dealt to the Washington Senators for the 1893 season, and he spent the final weeks of the 1892 season suspended or on the bench.

O'Rourke's final major league season came in Washington at age 42 as a player/manager. He played in 129 of the team's 130 games, posting a .287 batting average with 95 runs batted in. He served as the aging star of a team destined for last place, finishing with a dismal 40-89 record. Jim O'Rourke decided that it was time to retire from major league baseball, returning to Bridgeport with eight championships, a .313 career batting average, and 2,638 career hits, second only to Cap Anson.

O'Rourke attempted to fill his time with his legal practice, but he felt compelled to return to baseball in some capacity. In 1894, he tried a stint as a National League umpire, but he didn't enjoy the role. He then returned to the field as a semi-pro player while attempting to build his own team in Bridgeport. His venture resulted in the founding of the Bridgeport Victors, for whom O'Rourke played alongside Harry Herbert, an African-American player that would play on O'Rourke's teams for the next four seasons in a sport otherwise professionally reserved for whites. In 1896, O'Rourke joined the Victors with seven other teams in the Naugatuck Valley League, a forerunner of the Connecticut State League, which would operate as late as 1914 as the Eastern Association. In 1896, the forty-six-year-old O'Rourke batted .437 and led his team to the pennant as its catcher and manager. He would continue to play minor league baseball until the age of fifty-four, while also serving as an advisor to the National Association of Professional Base Ball Leagues and in a number of civic capacities such as Bridgeport Fire Commissioner. O'Rourke retired after his 1,999th minor league game in 1904.

At the same time, the New York Giants were approaching their first National League pennant since 1889, and manager John McGraw, as a way to pay homage to the pervious pennant winners, invited Jim O'Rourke to catch the clinching game. Thus, in 1904, O'Rourke returned to the major leagues to catch a final nine-inning game, hitting a single and scoring a run in the process at the age of fifty-four. To those that marveled at his ability to compete well into his fifties, O'Rourke identified two reasons: that he never drank or smoked, and that baseball was "the real elixir of life". He would return to catch one final minor league game between the New Haven Wings and Waterbury at the age of sixty-two.

Thereafter, O'Rourke remained in the business of baseball for several more years, but they were not always happy ones. The rise and demise of different minor leagues often put him at odds with his colleagues, and on at least one occasion he found himself in the position of having to impose a salary cap as President of the Connecticut State League. At the same time, members of his family were growing older, moving away, and sometimes passing away. Having survived his mother, his brother and his wife, Jim O'Rourke was still actively practicing law when he walked to and from the office on New Year's Day 1919 to consult with a client. He developed pneumonia and died seven days later at the age of sixty-eight. Twenty-six years later, Jim O'Rourke's plaque was installed at Cooperstown, a well-deserved tribute that was only too short to represent the totality of his importance to the game.

Major League Debut: April 26, 1872, for the Middletown Mansfields

Final Major League Game: September 22, 1904, for the New York Giants

Career Batting Average: .311; N.L. Batting Average Leader in 1884 (.347)

Career Hits: 2,643

Career Homeruns: 62; National Association HR Leader 1874, 1875; N.L.
HR Leader in 1880

Career Runs Scored: 1,729

Inducted to the Major League Baseball Hall of Fame: 1945

O'Rourke's Hall of Fame Plaque Reads:

> JAMES H. O'ROURKE
> "ORATOR JIM" PLAYED BALL UNTIL HE
> WAS PAST FIFTY, INCLUDING TWENTY-ONE
> MAJOR LEAGUE SEASONS. AN OUTFIELDER
> AND CATCHER FOR THE BOSTON RED
> STOCKINGS OF 1873, HE LATER WORE
> THE UNIFORMS OF THE CHAMPIONSHIP
> PROVIDENCE TEAM OF 1879, BUFFALO,
> NEW YORK AND WASHINGTON.

CHARLES GARDNER "OLD HOSS" RADBOURN

In 1854, the U.S. Congress passed the Kansas-Nebraska Act, an Act sponsored by Illinois Senator Stephen Douglas in order to support the construction of a transcontinental railroad in the Midwest, an action that would unite the east-west transcontinental elements of the nation while opening the Midwest to further settlement and farming prosperity. Celebration of the Act's passage was brief as, instead of immediately leading to prosperity, it led to Civil War. The Kansas-Nebraska Act relied upon a foundation of popular sovereignty, a doctrine that would have allowed each U.S. territory to determine the legality of slavery within its boundaries by popular vote. In consequence, the Act ran contrary to the Missouri Compromise, 1820 legislation that had established a boundary line for the existence of slavery within the United States. The result was Bloody Kansas, a series of violent clashes and tumultuous politics within the newly formed Kansas Territory, an expression of sectional clashes that would further devolve into the Civil War.

Also in 1854, on December 11, Charles Radbourn was born as the second of eight children to Charles Radbourn and his wife Caroline, English immigrants who had arrived in the United States only a few years earlier. In that pre-War era, while baseball held a significant role in American society, no ability to legitimately pursue the game professionally could have been anticipated. With their new country descending into divisive turmoil around them, there is no way that anyone in the Radbourn family could have looked at young Charlie and conceived that he would one day be heralded as the greatest of nineteenth century pitchers by aficionados of the national pastime.

Born in Rochester, New York, Charlie Radbourn was largely raised in Bloomington, Illinois. He attended the local school and helped to work his family farm. His pastimes were hunting and baseball. As he entered his teens, Charlie prepared to follow his father's professional footsteps as a butcher, and he began working regularly in a slaughterhouse. He also mirrored his father as a brakeman for the Indiana, Bloomington and Western Railway, routinely making the route to Indianapolis and back. For all of his work, he still enjoyed throwing a baseball against a wall of the family barn, and as he entered his twenties, he obtained a position on the local team, the Bloomington Reds, allowing him to make a bit of extra money on weekends and holidays.

Radbourn's baseball career almost never made it past the local level as he found himself in the midst of a game-fixing scandal involving the Reds' 4-1 loss to a Springfield team on September 1, 1976. In that game, Radbourn had one hit in four at-bats, but he also committed five errors in left field. The Reds committed fourteen errors in all, the local newspaper reported significant betting on the game, and three of the players, not including Radbourn, were seen drinking with known gamblers after the game. As part of its continuing investigating, the Bloomington paper interviewed Radbourn. He admitted to drinking heavily the night before the game and to speaking with two known gamblers in the saloon while doing so. Others who were in the saloon that night alleged that Radbourn told them he had been offered $25 to throw the game. Radbourn could not recall whether he had accepted the bribe while drunk. The following morning before the game, gamblers approached Radbourn again, offering $75 for him, his cousin, and a third Bloomington player. Radbourn refused that offer and reported it to the others who also refused it. As a result of the scandal and subsequent investigation, as professional baseball was in its infantile stage and required a reputation of legitimacy in order to attract spectators, the Reds' stockholders fired two players from the team, but Charlie Radbourn was permitted to stay, as his only possible involvement could be attributed to a state of inebriation.

Entering the 1877 season, Charlie began to pitch regularly and worked hard to develop a curveball. His highlight for the year may have been an exhibition game against Al Spalding's Chicago White Stockings, a game in which Charlie pitched very effectively in relief and left an impression on the professional team. For 1878, Charlie stepped beyond the confines of local familiarity and signed with the Peoria Reds, a professional barnstorming team. For them, he would play right field and serve as the change pitcher. In the nineteenth century, the change pitcher served as a secondary pitcher for a team, but there were no direct pitching substitutions. A team's manager, rather than stepping onto the field, would signal to a team's captain to order a position change. At that point, the primary pitcher would trade positions with the team's change pitcher, leaving the same nine men on the field. With regard to Charlie Radbourn's experience on the Peoria Reds, right field was used as the alternative position for the pitchers, so Charlie would start most of the games in right field and go to the pitcher's mound in relief as ordered. Those relief appearances were not rare, but they would have occurred in a minority of games as nineteenth century pitchers generally had the expectation to complete the games that they started. As a result, Radbourn's primary focus would be to prepare himself as a right fielder, and it seems that he did a serviceable job, batting .299 in 28 games.

In 1879, Charlie Radbourn moved again, this time to the Dubuque, Iowa, team of the Northwest League. Formed that same year, the League's organizer, Ted Sullivan, built the Northwest League with the intention of subordinating it to the National League, which has led many to consider it the first official minor league in baseball. Charlie played second base, outfield and change pitcher, and again he had an excellent season. In later years, Cap Anson would look back upon an August 4, 1879, exhibition between the Chicago White Stockings and the Dubuque team that ended in a 1-0 Dubuque victory and provide high praise of Radbourn's confounding curveball. Radbourn also batted .337 as Dubuque won the league's pennant, thereby paving his way to the major leagues.

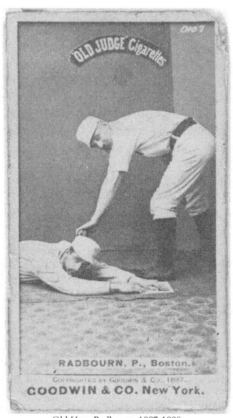

Old Hoss Radbourn, 1887-1890
Old Judge (N172)
Courtesy of Library of Congress PPOC

Radbourn signed with the major league Buffalo Bisons for the 1880 season to play second base, right field, and to serve as change pitcher. However, things did not go as planned as he injured his shoulder during spring training and, as a result, would never throw a single pitch for the Buffalo squad. Instead, his 1880 appearances were split with just three at second base and three in right field. He hit for only a .143 batting average and was released after just six games. Believing his baseball career to be over, Charlie returned to Bloomington to work as a butcher.

Time away from baseball helped Radbourn's shoulder to heal. Though he no longer planned to pursue baseball professionally, when the National League Providence Grays played an exhibition game against a local Bloomington team, Radbourn agreed to pitch, and his performance was enough to prompt continued interest from the National League. As a result, prior to the 1881 season, Radbourn received several telegrams of interest, but he did not answer any of them. Instead, it appears that a friend wrote to the Providence team while pretending to be Radbourn, negotiated a contract, and then convinced Radbourn to take the opportunity after the arrangements were made. Radbourn borrowed money to go to Hot Springs, Arkansas, to get into playing shape before reporting to spring training. As before, Charlie was to serve as change pitcher and to fill other positions on the field as needed. This time, however, he was healthy for the season and was able to play a vital role in Providence's second place finish. In all, Radbourn made 13 appearances at shortstop, one in centerfield, 24 in right field, and 41 as pitcher. He batted just .219, but he managed a 25-11 pitching record, which ranked him sixth in the league for wins and gave him the league's best win-loss pitching percentage. He also ranked eighth in the league with 117 strikeouts.

Radbourn's pitching success came in the underhanded era of major league baseball pitching. Radbourn frequently threw underhanded, but he was also known to mix in overhanded pitching once it was legalized in 1884. He actually pitched from a variety of angles, which is something that contributed to his success. He mixed a good fastball with an excellent curveball, a screwball and a changeup. Perhaps his most devastating weapon was his ability to vary the speed of his pitches, and he was known to be devastatingly unpredictable – in arm angle, pitch selection and speed – throughout his career. He also used strategies as a pitcher, developing ways to doctor the baseball and also pitching around strong hitters to get to weaker hitters in a lineup. There are even some reports that he would pitch both right and left-handed, which would only further confuse batters in the era before gloves were worn in the field because they would not have known

1881 Providence Grays

which hand the pitch was coming from until the pitch was delivered. To develop and maintain his arm strength, Radbourn practiced with an iron ball and developed a workout routine based on long-tossing.

Radbourn continued to pitch well for Providence in subsequent seasons. He posted a 33-19 record in 1882 and led the league in victories with a 48-25 record in 1883. That season he also posted 315 strikeouts, after leading the league with 201 the year before, and he pitched a no-hitter against Cleveland on July 25. 1883 also saw him post career highs in batting average (.289) and homeruns (3). However, of those two successful campaigns, Radbourn's finest single moment may have occurred on August 17, 1882, in a game in which he did not throw a single pitch. On that date, in what is considered by many to be the finest baseball game ever played, the Detroit Wolverines faced the Providence Grays in a contest that went scoreless into the eighteenth inning. Radbourn made a game-saving catch in right field in the fifteenth inning, but he was hitless in his first six at-bats. However, in the bottom of the eighteenth inning, he lifted a fly ball over a closed gate in the left field wall to end the game with a homerun. That same gate had been open only innings before, and if it had remained open, the Wolverine's left fielder likely would have made the necessary catch. Furthermore, the gate was at the point where the foul line met the wall, so protests erupted over whether Radbourn's blast was even fair. Nonetheless, the umpire maintained his initial call, and the Grays had an eighteen-inning victory because of Radbourn's only homerun of the season. Still, this, nor anything else Radbourn had previously accomplished, foreshadowed the greatness that he would achieve in 1884.

From its onset, there was not much about the 1884 that looked promising for Charlie Radbourn. Providence had finished in second and third place in the previous two seasons, and the pressure to finally win a pennant was mounting. Radbourn was also at odds with team ownership because he was dissatisfied with his salary. He had attempted to jump to the newly formed American Association in order to achieve a better salary in advance of the 1882 season, but instead stayed with Providence after being threatened with National League blacklisting. Following the tremendous success of his 1883 season, he requested a $4000 salary for the coming season, but he was granted only $2000. He was also to continue to be the change pitcher for the younger Charlie Sweeney, who made extra money for pitching the majority of Providence's games.

The season began in the manner that was to be expected. Through June, Sweeney and Radbourn basically shared the team's pitching load evenly through its first 47 games. At that point, Sweeney's arm appears to have gotten sore, perhaps because of his new overhanded pitching approach or the nature of his screwball, and he required rest that allowed him to pitch only in relief and forced Radbourn to serve as starting pitcher for 10 of the team's next 12 games. Radbourn then became upset again about his salary as he was not provided the same bonus pay that Sweeney had received when he had been the team's primary starter. During the ten games that he pitched during that stretch, Radbourn's normally excellent performance was merely mediocre, resulting in a 6-4 record, and newspaper accounts labeled him as "careless and indifferent." Then, on July 16, Radbourn lost to the Boston Beaneaters, and Providence suspended him for what appeared, based on slow pitching, a balk that resulted in key runs, and overall sloppy play, to be a less-than-sincere effort. Following the game, a fight broke out in the Providence clubhouse between Sweeney and Radbourn, with Radbourn being the instigator. Radbourn had fallen out of favor with the Providence Grays, but the situation would soon change again as Charlie Sweeney brought his own problems to the team.

Prior to his arm soreness, Sweeney had also pitched very well for the Providence Grays in 1884. On June 7, he had achieved a major league record with nineteen strikeouts in a single game, a record that would stand until broken by Roger Clemens' twenty strikeout game in 1986. However, following Radbourn's suspension, when he was reluctantly pressed back into regular service, Sweeney would fail his team because of his character rather than his ability. Only July 21, Providence had an exhibition game in Woonsocket that was to be followed by a morning practice and an afternoon game the following day. Sweeney reportedly drank throughout the course of the exhibition game. He then spent the night with a woman in Woonsocket, missed his team's morning practice, and was in poor condition for the afternoon game in which he was supposed to pitch. Still, with Radbourn on suspension, the team had to move forward with Sweeney as pitcher. The game progressed poorly for Sweeney, but in the fifth inning when the Providence manager signaled the captain to switch pitchers, Sweeney refused to leave the mound and pitched for another two innings. Following the seventh inning, Sweeney was told that he would be fined $50 if he did not leave the pitcher's mound. He response was to quit the team immediately, and he watched the rest of the game from the stands wearing civilian clothes as Providence was forced to finish with only eight players on the field. Sweeney left the game with two prostitutes, and the Grays banned him from the National League for the remainder of the season. Sweeney would instead pitch for the Union Association St. Louis Maroons. He helped them to win their pennant, and he returned to the National League in 1885 as the Maroons entered as a new NL team, but following 1884, Sweeney would never again be a dominant pitcher.

Sweeney's departure left Providence in desperate circumstances, and it was Radbourn who came to the rescue as he volunteered to start every game for the remainder of the season in exchange for receiving the pay for two pitchers and an exemption from the baseball reserve clause for the following season. Facing otherwise the likely complete collapse of their team, the Grays accepted with 51 games remaining. Radbourn started 41 of those games, winning 35 of them. As a result, the Providence Grays won the pennant, and Radbourn won the elite pitching triple crown. He finished the season with a 59-12 record, an earned run average of 1.38 and 441 strikeouts. In total, he had started 73 games, and he completed every one of them. He also entered games to record saves on two occasions. With little argument, Charlie Radbourn's 1884 season may stand as the best single season performance by any pitcher in baseball history. In fact, some accounts even attribute Radbourn with a sixtieth win as he was initially credited with a win for one of his relief appearances on July 28 because he was the Gray's best pitcher in that game, though he entered the game with a lead. While such a performance is credited as a save under modern rules, at the time, a scorekeeper had discretion in awarding the win, and under the rules of his day, that allowed Radbourn a 60-12 overall record. Further, as a result of their pennant victory, the Providence Grays moved on to face the New York Metropolitans in the very first World Championship Series. The Grays swept the three-game series, each game of which was a complete game victory by Charlie Radbourn.

Of course, Radbourn's superhuman 1884 performance did not come without a cost. Once he began his tremendous workload in the season's second half, Radbourn would often have tremendous arm pain, and he frequently struggled to lift his right arm, even for such mundane chores as combing his hair. He countered those challenges with massages and extended warm-ups. As, at 5' 9" and 168 lbs., Radbourn was of fairly average stature, the press marveled even further at his workload. When asked about fatigue in 1884, he reportedly responded incredulously, "Tired out tossing a little five-ounce baseball for two hours? I used to be a butcher. From four in the morning until eight at night I knocked down steers with a 25-pound sledge. Tired from playing two hours a day for ten times the money I used to get for sixteen hours a day?"

Following the season, the Providence Grays honored their promised to exempt Radbourn from the reserve clause, thereby allowing him to sign with any baseball team of his choosing, but they also offered him a lucrative contract, and he accepted, thereby pitching for them again in 1885. He posted a 25-21 record as the Grays fell to fourth place before he left to join the Boston Beaneaters in 1886. With the Beaneaters, Radbourn would pitch well, winning more than twenty games in three of his four seasons, but he would never again come close to his 1884 performance. Interestingly, with the Boston Beaneaters in 1886, Charlie Radbourn earned another distinction as that season's team photograph shows him extending his middle finger for the camera. While the gesture has been one of disrespect and contempt since the days of Ancient Greece and Ancient Rome, Radbourn's gesture is the earliest known offering of the finger by a public figure in a photograph.

Charlie Radbourn's final season of greatness came in 1890 as he posted a 27-12 record for Mike Kelly's Boston Reds of the Players' Association as they went on to win the pennant. After finishing third in the league for earned run average and fourth in the league for victories, when the Players' Association dissolved, Radbourn moved to the Cincinnati Reds of the National League in 1891 where he played for manager Tom Loftus, who had been Radbourn's manager so many years before in Peoria when he had first ventured into professional baseball. The season was a disappointment, both for Radbourn and the Cincinnati team. The Reds finished in a virtual tie for last place with a 56-81 record, and Radbourn was able to start only a career-low 23 games, finishing with a losing record of 11-13. Radbourn was granted a requested release on August 23, and at the age of thirty-six, he retired from baseball.

Radbourn returned to Bloomington to manage a billiard parlor and saloon that he had purchased in 1888. He married and had a son, and in 1893 and 1894 he made inquiries about returning to the major leagues. However, in the spring of 1894, he was shot in the face in a hunting accident, and he lost his left eye. Facially disfigured, and suffering partial paralysis and speech loss, Radbourn became a recluse in the back rooms of his saloon. He began to drink heavily, and he suffered severe mental and physical illnesses. In February 1897, a convulsion left Radbourn in a coma, and major league baseball's best single-season pitcher died away from the limelight at the age of 42.

Major League Debut: May 05, 1880, for the Buffalo Bisons

Final Major League Game: August 11, 1891, for the Cincinnati Reds

Win-Loss Record: 309-194

Career Earned Run Average: 2.68

Career Strikeouts: 1,830

Won the Pitching Triple Crown in 1884

Established the Single Season Record for Wins with 59 in 1884

Inducted to the Major League Baseball Hall of Fame: 1939

Radbourn's Hall of Fame Plaque Reads:

CHARLIE RADBOURNE
"OLD HOSS"
PROVIDENCE, BOSTON AND CINCINNATI
NATIONAL LEAGUE 1881 TO 1891. GREATEST
OF ALL 19TH CENTURY PITCHERS. WINNING
1884 PENNANT FOR PROVIDENCE, RADBOURNE
PITCHED LAST 27 GAMES OF SEASON, WON
26, WON 3 STRAIGHT IN WORLD SERIES.

AMOS WILSON RUSIE

When the Greek philosopher Heraclitus referred to the god Zeus as "the Thunderbolt that steers the course of all things," his metaphor was built upon the thunderbolt as a representation of awesome power and change. By the late nineteenth century, as professional baseball left its infancy, the wonder of electricity was better understood as Thomas Edison set to work building a legacy by electrifying America's major cities as the turn-of-the-century drew near. Though partly tamed, the power of the thunderbolt was still awe-inspiring as it transformed the life of modern man. At the same time, Amos Rusie, known as the Hoosier Thunderbolt, hurled his fastball through the air, overwhelming his opponents and exploding with a clap of thunder as it struck the catcher's mitt during a brilliant, but short, career that was one of the era's most impactful.

John McGraw once said of Amos Rusie's fastball, "You can't hit 'em if you can't see 'em." That simple aphorism provided the basis for Rusie's career: his fastball was his weapon of choice, and it largely left his opponents defenseless. Born in May 1871, the same month as the first major league baseball game was played between the Cleveland Forest Cities and the Ft. Wayne Kekiongas, Amos Rusie had a somewhat brief major league career that not only brought him success, but also established him as an icon of the 1890s and distinctly influenced the development of the sport. Connie Mack, whose eleven-year playing career was followed by fifty years as manager of the Philadelphia Athletics, identified Rusie as the hardest throwing pitcher that he ever saw. Indeed, Rusie's talent allowed him to achieve greatness within the game while also eclipsing it to become a known cultural figure, though his success would ultimately fade almost as quickly as it had been realized.

Amos was the second of four children, and it seems certain that his father, a Civil War veteran, was an important figure in his Indiana boyhood.

William Rusie had joined the 33rd Indiana Volunteer Infantry at the age of sixteen. Despite having lost a leg during his service, he provided for his family through consistent work as a brick mason and plasterer, and he remained a dynamic and productive man for sixty years following his military discharge. Similarly, Amos attempted to step from boyhood to manhood at the age of sixteen, leaving school to work in a factory and a furniture store while using his time after-hours to play on several of Indianapolis' semi-professional baseball teams. After initially being positioned in the outfield, Amos was soon given an opportunity as a relief pitcher, and from that point, the sixteen-year-old established himself as a star hurler. At the age of seventeen, while playing for the local Strum Avenue Never Sweats, Rusie had the opportunity to pitch against two major league teams, the Boston Beaneaters and the Washington Nationals, both of whom were on national tours. He shut out both teams, and he was promptly signed by the National League Indianapolis Hoosiers, who sent Amos to pitch a total of four minor league games with the Burlington Babies of the Central Inter-State League before bringing their young pitcher to the majors.

The eighteen-year-old's freshman season had some successes as he posted a 12-10 record with a shutout and 109 strikeouts in thirty-three total games, of which twenty-two were starts. Still, the 6'1", 200-pound, redheaded fireballer struggled for control of his fastball, walking 116 batters and posting an earned run average of 5.32. In total, Rusie was an unreliable pitcher on a below-average team, as the Hoosiers finished in seventh place with a 59-75 record and were dissolved at the season's end. As the Hoosiers folded, the National League reallocated its players to other teams, and Rusie was sent to the New York Giants, with whom he would play 427 games over the next eight seasons of his career.

In 1890, despite their first-place finish in the previous season, the Giants were in need of the eight former Hoosier players they had received in exchange for $60,000, as they had lost several of their star players to the newly formed Players' League. For Rusie, this meant instant opportunity, and he would go on to pitch in 67 games for New York that season, starting 62 games and completing 56, coming in second with 548.2 total innings for the year. As early as May 12th, Rusie also established himself as someone capable of pitching brilliance as he faced off against Kid Nichols in a game in which both pitchers threw scoreless baseball for the first twelve innings. Following a teammate's homerun in the top of the thirteenth, Rusie set Nichols' Beaneaters down for the complete game shutout victory. It was clear that Rusie's performance could not be considered a fluke as he had defeated the Beaneaters just three days earlier while allowing only six hits. Rusie became an instant celebrity in New York society. A drink was named after him, he was the subject of a vaudeville play, and he socialized with Lillian Russell, a famed and stunningly beautiful singer of operettas and musical theater. Rusie became known for his drinking and carousing, but throughout it all, he continued to pitch. In doing so, he finished fourth in the league with a respectable 2.56 earned run average and led the league with 341 strikeouts at a time when foul tips did not count as strikes, thereby requiring pitchers to get three called or swing-and-miss pitches to record an out. Rusie also managed to become an impactful offensive player, batting .278 with 28 runs batted in over 292 plate appearances. Nonetheless, Rusie's control continued to be a consistent and substantial issue. He led the league with 34 losses and 36 wild pitches while also recording 289 walks allowed, a major league record for a single season that has never been eclipsed. The Giants finished in sixth place.

When the Players' League dissolved at the end of its single season, many of the Giants' former stars returned to the team, but Rusie was not displaced. His talent and potential were simply too great. For the next two seasons, he started 57 and 62 games respectively, winning more than 30 games and posting more than 300 strikeouts in each. On July 31, 1891, Rusie pitched a no-hitter against John Montgomery Ward's Brooklyn Grooms. In addition to settling into his role as a star pitcher, Rusie was also trying to settle into a stable personal life with his marriage to May Smith while in Indiana for the 1890-91 offseason. Still, in both his personal and professional life, Rusie's control continued to be a concern. His drinking and party lifestyle continued, and he continued to lead the league with 262 and 270 walks over those next two years, thereby giving him three of the four highest single season walks allowed totals in baseball history. Rusie's lack of control came with a velocity that found Dick Buckley, his regular catcher, stuffing his glove with a piece of lead wrapped with a handkerchief and a sponge in an effort to reduce the resulting pain. In short, he presented a danger that was recognized by the entirety of the National League, which decided to alter the distance between the pitcher's mound to homeplate from 55 feet, 6 inches to 60 feet, 6 inches in an effort to protect its batsmen from the Hoosier Thunderbolt.

The additional five feet of pitching distance seemed to have little impact upon Rusie. In 1893, he posted a 33-21 record while completing 50 of the 52 games that he started. He also led the league with 208 strikeouts and 218 walks. 1894 became Rusie's finest season as he achieved what would eventually become known as pitching's triple crown with 36 wins, a 2.78 earned run average (in a year when the average was 5.33), and 195 strikeouts. While he also led the league once again with 200 walks, Rusie helped to lead the Giants to a second-place finish, which placed them in contention for baseball's first Temple Cup, a seven game postseason series between baseball's two best teams. Rusie helped New York to dominate its competition in that series, the Baltimore Orioles, on the way to a four-games-to-none series victory. Rusie pitched two complete game victories, giving up only one earned run in his eighteen innings, and he batted .429 for the series. Rusie had finally established himself as the best pitcher on the best team in major league baseball.

Unfortunately, the success that Rusie and the Giants had found could not be repeated in 1895. Though he led the league with 201 strikeouts and 4 shutouts while lowering his base on ball total to 159, Rusie appeared in fewer games and pitched less innings than at any point since his rookie season. While he was ninth in the league with 23 wins, he achieved only a 23-23 record, and the Giants sank to ninth place in the twelve-team league. In the midst of the tough season, team owner Andrew Freedman fined Rusie $200 of his $3000 salary, $100 for breaking curfew and $100 for lack of effort. Irate, Rusie refused to sign his contract for the 1896 season until the $200 was returned to him. Thus began a stand-off that saw Rusie sit out the entire 1896 season, after which he sued the Giants' owner for $5000 and release of his contract. While Freedman refused to concede to Rusie's demands, the National League's other owners, in fear of the safety of their contracts' reserve clause, raised $5000 and offered it to Rusie on the condition that he drop his suit. Rusie accepted the $5000 and returned to the New York Giants in 1897 with his regular $3000 salary.

Amos Rusie, 1895
Mayo's Cut Plug (N300)
Courtesy of Library of Congress PPOC

Rusie must have felt that all was right with the world as he returned to the diamond and his wife gave birth to a daughter, the couple's only child. While limited to only 38 games in 1897 due to an aching arm, he posted a 28-10 record, the best winning percentage of his career, and he led the league with a 2.54 earned run average. He was fourth in the league in strikeouts while allowing only 87 walks, but the control of his fastball was as dangerous as ever. In June, Rusie faced Hugh Jennings, who would eventually earn baseball's all-time record for being hit by pitches. A Rusie fastball struck Jennings in the head, and while accounts of the injury vary, many indicate that Jennings was unconscious for three to four days. While Rusie's 1897 return to baseball had been a success, that success was not total. The Giants finished in third place, nine and a half games behind the league leaders.

In 1898, while no longer pitching amongst the league leaders in any given category, Rusie once again set about building a good record before tragedy struck him in August. While trying to pick Chicago speedster Bill Lange off of first base, Rusie felt something snap in his shoulder. After taking five weeks off to allow his arm to heal, Rusie finished the season with a 20-11 record, but when he reported to spring training the following season, his arm was dead. Rusie blamed the damage on his snap pick-off move. He had also been struck by a line drive during the 1898 season, resulting in sustained problems with his hearing, so Rusie decided to step away from the game in order to reestablish his health. It was a decision that would cost him the entirety of the 1899 and 1900 seasons.

Along with Rusie's physical and professional problems came problems with his marriage. In January 1899, his wife filed for divorce while making allegations of drunkenness and abuse. The couple reconciled, but May would again file for divorce in early 1900, and her request was granted by the court. Devastated, Rusie begged his wife to return to him while promising to reform his excesses and his behavior. Rusie returned to live with his widower father in Indianapolis. Eventually May accepted her husband's promises, and the two were remarried just three months after their divorce had been finalized, but May had imposed an ultimatum. She demanded that her husband leave the New York Giants and New York City, as she detested city life and the corrupting effect that she believed it had upon her husband. Amos Rusie agreed.

Eligibility rules for the Hall of Fame require that a player must have competed in ten seasons, with further clarification that a single game counts as a "season" in the eyes of the Hall. Having begun in 1889, but having missed the entirety of three seasons, following a trade to Cincinnati where he played three games in 1901, Rusie only just met this qualification. In returning to the mound, he found that he could not reclaim his former greatness, striking out only six batters while allowing twenty-five runs in just twenty-two innings. The final game of his career was a June 9, 1901, loss to the New

York Giants. At the age of thirty, his major league career was over. Nonetheless, even in his failed attempted comeback with Cincinnati, Rusie acted as the thunderbolt that brought transformative change to baseball once again. In sending their former superstar to Cincinnati, the New York Giants had received a young pitcher named Christy Mathewson in return.

As his father had before him, Rusie answered the tragedy of his early life with continued hard work. Much of the fortune that he had made in baseball had been spent in New York or given away to family and friends. To support himself and his wife, Rusie went on to hold various jobs as a laborer in factories and a paper mill. He spent time as a ticket taker, a bottle layer, a gas fitter for a lighting company and a steamfitter for a shipyard. In 1921, Rusie was offered the position of "special officer" at the Polo Grounds by John McGraw, but his wife didn't enjoy their return to the city, and when she became ill, the couple relocated to the west coast.

With May confined to a wheelchair, Rusie purchased a chicken ranch, but it failed at the onset of the Great Depression. He was then severely injured in a 1934 car accident, and the couple fell behind on their house payments. The local *Seattle Post-Intelligencer* teamed with *The Sporting News* in an effort to fundraise, but they could not save the Rusie home. However, they did provide the couple with a small house and an income on which to live. After only a few years, with further declines in health, the couple moved in with their daughter and son-in-law. Amos Rusie passed away on December 6, 1942, two months after the death of his wife. It would be thirty-five more years before the Veterans Committee would elect him to Baseball's Hall of Fame.

Major League Debut: May 09, 1889, for the Indianapolis Hoosiers

Final Major League Game: June 09, 1901, for the Cincinnati Reds

Career Win-Loss Record: 245-174; N.L. Wins Leader in 1894

Career Earned Run Average: 3.07; N.L. Leader 1894, 1897

Career Strikeouts: 1,934; N.L. Leader 1890-1891, 1893-1895

Won Pitching Triple Crown 1894

Inducted to the Major League Baseball Hall of Fame: 1977

Rusie's Hall of Fame Plaque Reads:

> AMOS WILSON RUSIE
> "THE HOOSIER THUNDERBOLT"
> INDIANAPOLIS N.L., NEW YORK N.L.,
> CINCINNATI N.L., 1889-1895
> 1897-1898 AND 1901
> GENERALLY CONSIDERED FIREBALL KING OF
> NINETEENTH-CENTURY MOUNDSMEN. NOTCHED
> BETTER THAN 240 VICTORIES IN TEN-YEAR
> CAREER. ACHIEVED 30-VICTORY MARK FOUR
> YEARS IN ROW AND WON 20 OR MORE GAMES
> EIGHT SUCCESSIVE TIMES. LED LEAGUE IN
> STRIKEOUTS FIVE YEARS AND LED OR TIED
> FOR MOST SHUTOUTS FIVE TIMES.

SAMUEL LUTHER "BIG SAM" THOMPSON

Sam Thompson's origins are as deeply American as those of baseball itself. His maternal great-grandfather, John McPheeters, served in the Revolutionary War, possibly under the Virginia regiment commanded by Commander William Washington, the second cousin of George Washington, and James Monroe or as part of the Overmountain Men, a famed group of frontiersmen who brought a turning point to the American Revolution with their victory at the Battle of King's Mountain. Following the Revolution, McPheeters settled in Indiana, a newly formed territory as of 1800, and it seems he set to work as a distiller. Years later, McPheeters' granddaughter Rebecca married Jesse Thompson, and the two began their family, which eventually numbered eleven children, in Danville, Indiana. Sam, the fifth child, was born before his father began his service in the 63rd Indiana Volunteers during the Civil War. Jesse purportedly learned the game of baseball from other soldiers during his war service, and when he and other soldiers were discharged to return to Danville, they brought the game of baseball with them.

Jesse taught the game to his six sons, each of whom grew to impressively healthy frontier physiques of more than six feet and 200 pounds. Each of the Thompson boys played for the Danville Browns, one of four amateur baseball teams in their town, establishing their skills in the game in front of excited audiences drawn from the surrounding area. Still, baseball was a pastime rather than a profession, and each of the Thompson boys found work in their community in professions ranging from druggist to baker. Sam found work as a carpenter, and it was that profession that found him repairing a roof when a baseball scout named Dan O'Leary came to town. O'Leary was looking for local talent while seeking to schedule exhibition games for the Indianapolis team that he represented. After convincing Sam to leave his roofing job to play, O'Leary scheduled an exhibition with the Danville Browns. Sam's hitting, which included two homeruns, led Danville to a 9-0 victory, and Sam was immediately signed to a professional contract with an Evansville, Indiana, team in the newly formed Northwestern League in July 1884.

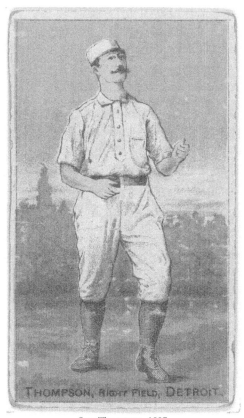

Sam Thompson, 1887
Buchner Gold Coin (N284)
Courtesy of Library of Congress PPOC

Sam joined the Evansville team for the second half of its 1884 season, but his experience would last only five games before the Northwestern League folded in early August. Nonetheless, Sam played well enough to secure a new contract with the Indianapolis Hoosiers of the Western League, which formed in 1885. In Indianapolis, Sam batted .321 in 30 games, and the Hoosiers were the premier Western League team, but Sam's luck seemingly faltered again as the league folded in mid-June. However, the end of Sam's play in Indianapolis would also be the beginning of his major league journey.

Regulations of the day allotted major league teams a ten-day window to bid for the services of players from a disbanded team. The Detroit Wolverines promptly arrived in Indianapolis, following the Hoosiers' disbanding, intent on inquiring Jim Keenan and Larry McKeon, the Hoosiers' catcher and principal pitcher, but they found themselves outbid by the Cincinnati Reds. Intent on reaping some benefit from the Hoosiers' demise, the Wolverines quickly placed bids on Sam Thompson and the remaining members of the team's starting lineup, and they also offered to organize a fishing trip for the players on Lake Huron. It was not until they were on the lake that the players realized that the captain had been told not to bring them back to land until the ten-day window had closed so that no other ballclub would be able to bid for their services. According to Thompson, the players were well-cared for on the boat, and upon reaching shore, they each signed a contract with Detroit. It was not until afterwards that they were allowed access to the various contract bids that had been sent to them through the mail.

Sam joined the Wolverines in mid-season, and he delivered a hit against future Hall of Famer Tim Keefe in his first at-bat, though he split his pants while racing for second because the Wolverines had not been able to supply a uniform that would fit him properly. The National League, however, fit Thompson well from the start. In the 63 games that he was able to play with Detroit in 1885, he posted a .303 batting average while finishing third in the league with 7 homeruns, tenth in the league with 9 triples, and fifth in the league with 24 outfield assists. The team also moved from a last-place standing at the time of Thompson's acquisition to a sixth-place finish in the eight-team league with a record of 41-67.

The following season saw an immediate turn-around in Detroit's competitiveness as they acquired the entirety of the Buffalo Bisons' infamous "Big Four" infield featuring Dan Brouthers, Jack Rowe, Hardy Richardson and Deacon White. Thompson also played a significant role on the team by ranking eighth in the league with a .310 batting average while finishing fourth with 13 triples, sixth with 8 homeruns, ninth with 101 runs scored and third with 89 runs batted in. As a result, the Wolverines reached a second-place finish with an 87-36 record, the best winning percentage of any major league team to ever play in Detroit. Nonetheless, despite the significant team and individual successes of the 1886 Wolverines, the season merely served as an appetizer for what was to come.

Sam Thompson, 1887-1890
Old Judge (N172)
Courtesy of Library of Congress PPOC

In 1887, the Wolverines completed spring training in Macon, Georgia, and then set about a six-week series of exhibition games to prepare for the season. The strategy seemed spectacularly successful. Thompson, at age 27, distinguished himself as a superstar by leading the league with a .372 batting average, 203 hits, 23 triples, and a major league record 166 runs batted in while also posting his first 10 homerun season. The rest of the Wolverines followed suit, and the team claimed the National League pennant with a 79-45 record. At 969 to 714, the Wolverines also outscored their opposition by more than 250 runs throughout the course of the season, and they also led the league in batting average, runs scored, and slugging. Following the season, Wolverines' owner Fred Stearns challenged the St. Louis Browns of the American Association to a series of contests to determine unquestioned supremacy of the baseball world. The resulting 15-game 1887 World Series involved games in Pittsburgh, Brooklyn, New York City, Philadelphia, Boston, Washington D.C., Baltimore Chicago, Detroit and St. Louis. The Wolverines won the series and its trophy, the Dauvray Cup, with their eighth victory in Game Eleven, but the series was played through to its conclusion with Detroit winning ten of the fifteen games. Sam Thompson hit two homeruns in Detroit's Game Eight victory and led all hitters from both teams with a .362 average for the series.

Unfortunately, neither Thompson nor the Wolverines could repeat their greatness in 1888. Plagued with a sore arm throughout the season, Sam was limited to only 56 games, and he suffered a substantial reduction in every offensive category. Other Wolverines also experienced reduced production, though not as dramatically, and the team only managed a 68-63 season, placing them fifth in the league of eight teams. Furthermore, the failure to meet expectations negatively impacted the team's financial returns, and ownership determined that the team was no longer viable. The Wolverines were dissolved at season's end, and their players were sold off to other organizations. Purchased for $5000 cash, on October 16, Sam Thompson found himself a member of the Philadelphia Quakers. Despite the transition to another city's ballclub, upon Sam's 1888 marriage to Ida Morasha, the couple decided to maintain their home in Detroit.

Philadelphia offered Sam Thompson a new beginning, and he responded. Despite batting well below his career average at .296, Thompson scored 103 runs while driving in 111 and hitting his career-high 20 homeruns, which he combined with 24 stolen bases to become baseball's first 20/20 player. Thompson must have also served as a sort of mentor to Philadelphia's younger players, such as 21-year-old Ed Delahanty, and the Quakers team finished fourth with a 63-64 record. The 1890 season brought a better result as the Quakers rebranded themselves as the Philadelphia Phillies and finished in third place at 78-53. As the Players' League attracted many of the sport's brightest stars, Thompson stuck in the National League and finished as the leading batman in hits (172) and doubles (41) while collecting 102 runs batted in and 116 runs scored though hitting only four homeruns for the season. Thompson was similarly productive over the two subsequent seasons as the Phillies established themselves as a fixture in the league's fourth place.

While 1893 brought the Phillies' third consecutive fourth place finish, it brought a resurgence in Sam Thompson's performance. In addition to leading the league with 37 doubles and a career-high 222 hits, Thompson also posted a career-high in runs (130) and totals in batting average (.370) and runs batted in (122) that were his highest since his break-through 1887 season. The disparity between the Phillies' finish and Thompson's own performance led the generally well-tempered outfielder to lash out at management at the season's end. In October, he announced that he would resign with the team because of ownership's unwillingness to spend money in support of their players. Luckily, team ownership was both receptive of Thompson's criticism and eager to retain him. After conceding to improved travel arrangements for the team, the Phillies were able to finalize a contract agreement with Thompson in March 1894, leading to a season of one of greatest offensive team achievements in baseball history.

That season, Sam Thompson posted a career-high .415 batting average but did not even lead his own team in hitting. That honor went to Tuck Turner, who finished with a .418 average, but that was only one half of the great Phillies' achievement of 1894. Ultimately, all four of the team's outfielders finished the season with an average above .400 as Ed Delahanty and Billy Hamilton finished at .405 and .413 respectively. Never before nor since have major league teammates shared a .400 season. Thompson also led the league with runs batted in (146) and slugging percentage (.696) despite missing a month of the season, during which a portion of his left pinkie finger was amputated. Speculation has led to the theory that his injury was caused by catching baseballs with his left hand before fielders' gloves became a regular feature of the game. Regardless, Thompson returned to hit for the cycle on August 17, as part of a month where the Phillies scored 312 runs, the major league record for runs in a single month. Such a landmark offensive season must have helped to soften the reality of yet another fourth place Philadelphia finish.

1895 was Thompson's final superstar offensive season. He batted .392 while leading the league in homeruns (18), runs batted in (165), total bases (352) and slugging percentage (.654) while striking out only 11 times. His season average of 1.39 runs batted in per game is second in baseball only to his own 1.44 runs batted in per game average of the previous season. 1896 saw him hit nearly .300 (.298) with 100 runs batted in and 103 runs scored. At the same time, his outfield play had never been finer as he led the league in outfield assists, double plays turned as an outfielder, and fielding percentage as an outfielder, each for the second time in his career. Unfortunately, the Phillies struggled despite his play, and the team slipped to eighth place in the league.

Thompson would never again play a full professional season of baseball. An injury-shortened season of just 3 games in 1897 was followed by only 14 games in 1898. Skeptical of the Phillies being able to compete for a pennant, at odds with management and tormented by back pain, Thompson retired in May 1898, despite still being effective at the plate with a .349 batting average, 9 extra-base hits and 15 runs batted in over the course of just 63 at-bats. As the United States began a war with Spain that would extend American imperialism beyond the boundaries of the continent, Sam Thompson stepped away from professional baseball and returned home to Detroit.

As Detroit grew as an industrial city, Thompson served as a U.S.

Marshall and a bailiff for the federal courts. He also invested in real estate, and by all accounts he was able to live comfortably. His enthusiasm for baseball continued, and he remained active by playing games with the Detroit Athletic Club. Then, in 1906, Sam Thompson returned to the field as a major league player for the final time after he volunteered to play for the Detroit Tigers, whose outfielders were suffering from a variety of mid-season injuries. Accounts report that Thompson fans flooded the stadium as he batted .226 with 7 hits, 3 runs and 4 runs batted in over the course of 8 games. Detroit sportswriter Paul Bruske noted that Thompson could still make the throw from right field to home plate "on a line," and that he still featured speed on the bases. Temporarily completing another all-Hall of Fame outfield with Ty Cobb and Sam Crawford, Thompson also became the oldest major league player to hit a triple at age 46.

Moving once again into baseball retirement, Thompson remained a beloved figure in Detroit. His reputation remained that of a superb hitter, an excellent defensive outfielder, and a fine gentleman. Throughout his long and pronounced career, he was never involved in a fight, ejected from a game, or received any suspension.

In 1922, at the age of 62, Thompson was working as an election inspector on November 7th when he was stricken by a heart attack. He was promptly taken home for rest, but a second fatal attack occurred later in the day. Days later, the factories, business and courts of Detroit ceased work as the city observed his funeral.

In a game that requires teams to score more runs than their opponents in order to win, there is a case that Sam Thompson is one of the most skilled batsmen to ever play the game. He still holds the career record for most runs batted in per game (.923) and for the most runs batted in for a single month (61). Of all the players of the nineteenth century, only he batted in more than 150 runs in a single season, and he did so twice (1887 and 1895). In an eleven-year stretch, he only once failed to score 100 runs in a season, and that was during the 1888 season in which he was limited to only 56 games. However, more so than numbers, it may be the words of Bill Watkins, Thompson's manager with the Detroit Wolverines, that best captures the nature of Sam Thompson's career play: "He was a fine fielder and had a cannon arm and will live in my memory as the greatest natural hitter of all time."

Major League Debut: July 02, 1885, for the Detroit Wolverines

Final Major League Game: September 10, 1906, for the Detroit Tigers

Career Batting Average: .331; N.L. Batting Champion in 1887

Career Homeruns: 126; N.L. Leader 1889, 1895

Career Runs Batted In: 1,305; N.L. Leader 1887, 1894, 1895

Inducted to the Major League Baseball Hall of Fame: 1974

Thompson's Hall of Fame Plaque Reads:

SAMUEL LUTHER THOMPSON
DETROIT N.L., PHILADELPHIA N.L.
1885-1898; DETROIT A.L. 1906
ONE OF THE FOREMOST SLUGGERS OF
HIS DAY. LIFETIME BATTING AVERAGE
.336. BATTED BETTER THAN .400 TWICE.
GREAT CLUTCH HITTER. COLLECTED
200 OR MORE HITS IN A SEASON THREE
TIMES. TOPPED N.L. IN HOME RUNS AND
RUNS BATTED IN TWICE.

JAMES LAURIE "DEACON" WHITE

Canton, NY, is located approximately 175 miles from Cooperstown, but it took James White 166 years to traverse the distance. Having played during professional baseball's infancy, White would be frustrated at the fact that he was not invited to the Hall of Fame's opening ceremonies in 1939, and he would not actually be admitted to baseball's exclusive fraternity until 2013. However, the delay of White's embrace by the Hall is not evidence that he was anything less than supremely qualified for the honor that he received. Instead, it is a testament to three factors that aligned to postpone White's induction until the appropriate moment, three factors that are fundamental to the continued importance of baseball's history to today's game.

First, and perhaps most simply, by the time that the Hall opened its doors, Deacon White was 91 years old and was already a distant figure of baseball's past. Those who witnessed his career firsthand could not attest to his greatness in a widespread way, and as White built his playing career with a significant number of organizations, he was not embedded as foundational to any single long-standing team or league. Thus, his in-game greatness and the consistency of his long career did not serve White. Instead, the public focused on honoring the two generations of players that followed him. Secondly, the objective statistics that White accumulated during his career were not favorable in direct comparison to players of later times. While a .312 career batting average was excellent, it was not exceptional; 2067 career hits was not 3000; and 24 homeruns and 70 stolen bases were exceeded in outstanding single-season performances rather than being viewed as Hall of Fame career totals. In 1939, baseball still needed to mature to the point of viewing player performances contextually within their given eras and circumstances. Once advanced metrics and contextualized statistical comparisons were applied to White's career, it became evident that he not only belonged in Cooperstown, but that he had accumulated statistical achievements superior to those of many other players who had already been deservingly inducted.

Finally, the Hall of Fame Class of 2013 was one that called for the induction of Deacon White. As voters considered their ballots for that year, they were confronted by many names that were integrally linked to what had already become known as baseball's Steroid Era. Most prominently, in their first year of consideration, Barry Bonds and Roger Clemens, each clearly deserving of Hall induction based strictly on his unprecedented performance achievements, forced questions about the moral and ethical threshold for election. Of the 37 living players that appeared on the ballots, none received the number of votes necessary for Hall entrance. Instead, Deacon White was selected by the Veterans Committee as the single player who would be inducted that year. He was clearly a throwback to baseball's professional origins, a time when its competition was unadulterated and the game was intrinsically tied to American character. Deacon had been so nicknamed because of his strong moral code and the respect that his teammates and opponents accorded him.

In short, in addition to serving as a reminder of how modern baseball relies upon a foundation built generations ago, in 2013 White was employed as evidence that the modern game is also still accountable to legacies dating back more than a century.

The life of James White is amazingly intertwined with the development of the United States. Descended from a family traceable to colonial America, James was born in Caton, NY on December 2, 1847. Neither the Civil War nor the Mexican-American War had yet been conceived, and Iowa had just been accepted as the twenty-ninth state. Raised in a large family, he did not play baseball until 1865, at which time he learned it from a returning Union soldier, very possibly his older brother LeRoy who had served in the War's final year. Thus, like most of America, the urban game of baseball was brought to White's rural community because interactions during the Civil War had pollinated soldiers from such communities with a passion for what had become a preferred pastime with easy-to-teach, standardized rules.

James played on a local Caton team in 1866, and the next year he joined his brother LeRoy in playing for a team in nearby Corning. Then, in 1868, the brothers moved to Cleveland to join the semi-professional Forest City Base Ball Club. There, James began to establish himself as the best player on a team comprised mostly of unpaid locals. He played shortstop, catcher and pitcher, playing all 23 games of the season while hitting 7 homeruns and scoring 73 runs. White missed the first half of the 1869 season, possibly because he returned home to New York to work the family farm, but he ultimately played in 15 games for Cleveland, and he returned to the team again for the 1870 season. By that time, the Forest City team was much improved, having employed more semi-professional players, but they finished only 26-11, ranking them seventh of the eleven prominent 1870 base ball clubs. Still, White excelled, batting for 184 total bases in the 37 games while also pitching 74 innings with a 1.06 earned run average.

In 1871, the National Association of Professional Base Ball Players was created on St. Patrick's Day to separate professional baseball teams from the many amateur teams that received what was still largely local interest in the game. The Cleveland Forest Citys were one of the nine charter organizations of the league, paying ten dollars in dues to join. Newly married and playing alongside his brother Elmer, James White was on hand for the Forest Citys' game in Fort Wayne, IN, on the National Association's Opening Day on May 4. The honor of playing in the first professional baseball game had been decided by coin flip, and the distinction was supposed to go to the Boston Red Stockings and the Washington Olympics. However, that game was rained out, and by default James White became the first batter in a professional baseball game when he led off against the Fort Wayne Kekiongas at Hamilton Field, a former Civil War camp, at 3 o'clock on a rainy afternoon in front of a few hundred spectators. He doubled in his first at-bat, earning the first hit and the first extra-base hit in professional baseball, on his way to a 3 for 4 day. He then became part of baseball's first double-play as he was caught too far from second base when the next batter hit a fly ball to center field. In the bottom half of the inning, White also recorded professional baseball's first catch on a pop-up into foul territory from the Kekiongas' leadoff man. The Forest Citys lost 2-0, but the low-scoring affair, an anomaly in that age of baseball, became the national representation of what professional baseball would offer. A reporter sent the following to be published in the *New York Herald*: "The finest game of base ball ever witnessed in this country was played on the grounds of the Kekiongas of this city this afternoon, the playing throughout being without precedent in the annals of base ball, and the members of both clubs establishing beyond doubt their reputations as among the most perfect ball players in the United States." Likewise, the local *Fort Wayne Gazette* reported, "This is undoubtedly the best game on record. We know of nothing like it that has ever happened before. Just think of it, only two runs made in nine full innings!"

One week later, the Forest Citys also lost their home opener, despite a James' solitary homerun of the season. Overall, the opening professional season was a challenging one for the Cleveland team, ultimately ending with them in eighth place of nine teams with a 10-19 record. On the other hand, James White's success continued as he caught all 29 games of the season while batting .322 with 21 runs batted in and 40 runs scored. The 1872 season was similar in that the Forest Citys finished seventh, with a 6-16 record, in an expanded league of eleven teams. The team disbanded at season's end.

Tragedy had struck James White even before the season began when his teammate and brother Elmer died of tuberculosis on March 17, exactly one year from the day of the National Association's founding, thereby becoming the first professional baseball player to die. Nonetheless, James was ready when the season opened two months later. Despite the lack of team success, White played in all 22 season games, batting .339 with 22 runs batted in and 21 runs scored. He was named captain and manager for the team's final few games, during which the players were no longer under contract and instead played as a cooperative, splitting the gate receipts. The *New York Clipper* wrote of him, "We have never known him to growl at an umpire, and his record for integrity is untarnished by even a suspicion," thereby beginning to lay the national foundation for the recognition of outstanding behavior and moral conduct that became synonymous with White throughout the remainder of his career.

Following the dissolution of the Forest Citys, White intended to retire from baseball, returning to his New York home. However, the Boston Red Stockings, having lost their catcher after winning the 1872 National Association championship, lured him from retirement, reportedly with a salary of $1500. Still, White delayed reporting to the Red Stockings and almost did not report at all. During the offseason, he had accepted the religion of the Seventh Day Adventists, and in at time when professional athletes were stereotyped for poor moral conduct, he was concerned about whether he could live in accordance with his faith while playing professional ball. Ultimately, White decided that it was possible for a man to be a reputable Christian baseball player, and he reported for the 1873 season in which he would lead the league with 60 games played and 77 runs batted in while finishing third in batting with a .392 average. The Boston team won its second consecutive National Association championship with a record of 43-16-1. The *New York Clipper* named White the league's top catcher, again shining a spotlight on him as, "… a thoroughly honest and reliable player, and he is one whose daily habits of life show that his honesty is not simple policy, but a principle inherent in the man." White achieved his notoriety as a catcher at a time when catchers largely wore no protective equipment or gloves. As a result, the catching position was stationed several feet behind the batter so that the catcher would not suffer impacts from foul balls, and catchers were not expected to catch pitches cleanly. However, White was known for advancing towards homeplate during the pitch and catching balls cleanly, thereby putting him in a position to prevent baserunners from advancing.

White returned to Boston in 1874 with his salary raised to $1800. He began playing the season in right field but was eventually installed as the full-time catcher. He played in 70 team games, and while his batting average dropped to .301, he scored 75 runs while batting in 52, and he tied for second in the league with three homeruns. Again, the *New York Clipper* named him the league's best catcher, and the Boston Red Stockings won their third consecutive National Association championship with a 52-18 record.

Boston won its opening game in 1875 and never lost its hold on first place, ultimately winning its fourth consecutive championship with a 71-8-3 record. White split most of his time between catcher and right field due to occasional injury, but he offered another spectacular season, leading the league with 80 games played while batting in 60 runs and scoring 76. White won his first batting title with a .376 average, and he was awarded what was, very possibly, baseball's first Most Valuable Player award – a sterling silver water pitcher inscribed "Won by Jim White as most valuable player to Boston team, 1875." The award also served as a sort of parting gift to White, who, largely for considerations of salary, had signed an agreement during the season to leave the Red Stockings in order to play with the Chicago White Stockings in 1876.

In addition to changing teams, along with the rest of professional baseball, White was changing leagues. The National Association had existed for five seasons as a loose confederation of teams that did not truly answer to any centralized authority or league office. Any professional team that paid league dues could join the league, creating their own schedules and playing against the opponents of their own choosing. Frustrated in the fact of constant instability, members of eight charter franchises met to create the new National League, and the National Association was dissolved. The key instigator of the change was William Hulbert, owner of the Chicago White Stockings, who was facing consequences for his signing of James White and others during the season while they were playing with their previous teams. Building a new league helped him and his players to avoid repercussions for their business practices, and the new league also brought new centralization and authority and standardization to strengthen the professional sport. White played all 66 White Stockings games, and he led the league with 60 runs batted in while batting .343. No major league player would again lead the league in runs batted in while primarily playing the catching position until Roy Campanella did so in 1953, more than 75 years later. Behind White's lead, Chicago won the first National League pennant with a record of 52-14.

Deacon White, 1887
Buchner Gold Coin (N284)
Courtesy of Library of Congress PPOC

Before the 1877 season began, White signed to play with the Boston Red Caps and returned to the east coast. While doing some preseason coaching with Harvard's team, White was shown a model for a mask to be worn by catchers, and he decided to wholeheartedly endorse the invention. He would direct a blacksmith in the crafting of his own version of the mask, one that he could introduce to major league play. However, that year, he played mostly right field and first base, catching only on occasion, including for games pitched by his brother Will, allowing the duo to become the first sibling battery in major league history. At the plate, White delivered the finest season of his career. In 59 games, he led the league with 103 hits, 11 triples, 49 runs batted in and a .387 batting average while also scoring 51 runs and ranking third in the league with 2 homeruns. The Red Caps won the pennant with a 42-18 record, providing White with his fifth consecutive championship season. He was also beginning to become known throughout the league as Deacon as a result of his continued upstanding conduct and devotion to his faith.

After he briefly considered retirement to tend to the family farm, White decided to join the Cincinnati Reds with his brother Will in 1878, and he would stay with that club for the next three seasons. In addition to playing, White would help a rookie named Mike Kelly break in at the catcher's position. The Reds did not perform as well as had been hoped. After finishing in a close second place to the Boston team in 1878, Cincinnati slipped to fifth place with a 43-37 record in 1879 before dropping to last place in 1880 with a 21-59 record. At the plate, Deacon White performed well. His best Cincinnati season came in 1879 when he batted .330 with 52 runs batted in, both numbers good enough for fifth place in the league. In the same season, he served as the team's captain and, briefly, as its manager, though his managerial stint was ended when he refused to read aloud a degrading note that ownership had sent to the players. White played in only 35 of his team's 80 games in 1880, and for the first time in his career he batted under .300, finishing at .298. He also found himself at odds with team management when, towards the end of September, ten dollars was deducted from his pay as a fine for his baserunning without White being informed in advance. At the end of the season, the Cincinnati team was ejected from the National League for selling alcoholic beverages at their games and for renting out their field for Sunday games. Deacon White transitioned once again, this time signing with the Buffalo Bisons, for whom he would play the next five seasons.

In 1881, White played first base, second base, third base and outfield in addition to serving as backup catcher. He would become the regular third baseman during the 1882 season, from that point only serving as the team's relief catcher. The move to Buffalo and playing for manager Jim O'Rourke revitalized his career, and White played nearly every game for the team while raising his batting average and run production. The team performed respectably for White's first four seasons with them, recording winning records and finishing between third and fifth place in the league. In 1882, White and his wife had their only child, a daughter.

Entering the 1885 season, White was conflicted about continuing his career in baseball because of news that the National League might begin to permit games on Sundays. The Bisons' performance on the field did not help the situation as they descended to last place in the league amidst financial problems and discord between management and the players. While White played a strong third base and hit well throughout the course of the season, batting .292 with 57 runs batted in and 54 runs scored, the Bisons organization was purchased for $7000 by the Detroit Wolverines so that they could acquire Buffalo's star players. However, when White and other members of the Bisons began to suit up for the Wolverines, other teams protested that they should not be allowed to be transitioned to another team during the course of the season. When the league president agreed, White and the other players refused to rejoin the Bisons and embarked on a fishing trip on Lake Erie instead of playing the season's final games.

In 1886, White was legally acquired by the Wolverines and played the first of three seasons with them. He was again praised for his play at third, this time while playing in a career-high 124 games at age 38. White also contributed strong run production, batting .289 and scoring 65 runs while finishing eighth in the league with 76 runs batted in. The Wolverines finished in second place.

Deacon White, 1887-1890
Old Judge (N172)
Courtesy of Library of Congress PPOC

At age 39, White entered the 1887 season as the oldest player in the major leagues, but while he was reduced to a still-respectable 111 games played, his production improved. Batting .303, he hit 20 doubles, 11 triples, and 3 homeruns while scoring 71 runs, driving in 75, and stealing 20 bases. The Wolverines won the pennant with a 79-45 record and then undertook a fifteen-game World Series against the St. Louis Browns. White batted only

.207 in the series, but the Wolverines won it handily, finishing with a post-season record to deliver Detroit's first World Series Championship.

While White remained remarkably consistent in his age-40 1888 season, the Detroit Wolverines did not. White played in 124 games, finishing sixth in the league with a .298 batting average, seventh in doubles with 22, and fifth in runs batted in with 71. However, the team sank to fifth place with a 68-63 record, and financial strain caused them to sell off several of their star players. However, White's contract was not sold, and the Detroit team was disbanded. Believing that he was free to determine the next step in his career, White purchased an ownership interest in the Buffalo Bisons, he moved his family to Buffalo, and he was named club president as he prepared to play for the Bisons in 1889. Days later, he was notified that Detroit had transferred his contract to the Pittsburgh Alleghenies. Thereafter, White entered negotiations with the Alleghenies, and he eventually accepted $1250 for his release rights and a monthly $500 salary. When asked by a reporter about that agreement that both he and teammate Jack Rowe had accepted, White replied, "We appreciate the money, but we ain't worth it. Rowe's arm is gone. I'm over 40 and my fielding ain't so good, though I can still hit some. But I will say this. No man is going to sell my carcass unless I get half." In keeping with that prediction, White proceeded to have the worst season of his career, batting .253 with 35 runs scored and 26 runs batted in. The Alleghenies finished fifth in the league with a losing record.

In 1890, frustrations over players' contracts and treatment by ownerships led to the creation of the Players' League, and White left the Alleghenies to play with the Players' League Buffalo Bisons, in which he held an ownership interest. White would suffer some criticism for facilitating the team's sale to capitalist interests in Buffalo, and the team entered into the season without expectations to be competitive. Indeed, the Bisons finished in last place with a 36-96 record. At age 42, White played in his final major league season, batting .260 with 62 runs scored and 47 runs batted in. On July 9th, White pitched in his second major league game, the first time he had pitched since a single outing in 1876. He allowed 8 runs in 8 innings. His final major league game came on October 4th, as the Bisons were shutout by the Brooklyn Ward's Wonders.

In July 1891, White joined the Elmira Gladiators of the New York-Pennsylvania League as a player/manager/captain. He batted .229 in ten games before ending his baseball career for good.

Following his retirement, White settled in Buffalo where he owned a livery stable and ground lenses for the family's optometry business. He also helped to incorporate the Advent Christian Church of Buffalo. In 1909, White and his wife moved to Mendota, Illinois, where their daughter was attending Mendota College. The Whites became head residents at the school's young ladies' dormitory until 1912. Deacon White passed away at age 91 on July 7, 1939, while living with his daughter and her family.

During his major league career, Deacon White played all nine positions. He particularly distinguished himself as a catcher, arguably the best of the barehanded era, and later as a third baseman. His granddaughter would later remember his broken and misshapen hands, the result of years of punishment through barehanded play. In addition to being one of the best defensive players in baseball's early years, he also managed two decades of strong and amazingly consistent offensive production. At the time of his retirement, he ranked second in career runs batted in, as well as fourth in games played, at-bats, hits and total bases. His average career offensive numbers, when projected over a 162-game season, present a .312 batting average with 118 runs scored and 103 runs batted in. Additionally, Deacon White's reputation, in the early days when baseball drew criticism for professionalizing itself, was beyond reproach. His granddaughter recalls that, in the final years of his life, White offered comments and criticism to neighborhood children playing baseball and listened to the game on his radio while comfortably rocking in his chair.

Major League Debut: May 4, 1871, for the Cleveland Forest Citys

Final Major League Game: October 4, 1890, for the Buffalo Bisons

Career Batting Average: .312; NA Batting Champion 1875, NL Batting
Champion 1877

Career Hits: 2,067

Career Runs Batted In: 988; NA Leader 1873, NL Leader 1876-77

Inducted to the Major League Baseball Hall of Fame: 2013

White's Hall of Fame Plaque Reads:

JAMES LAURIE WHITE
"DEACON"
CLEVELAND, N.A., 1871-72
BOSTON, N.A., 1873-75; CHICAGO, N.L., 1876
BOSTON, N.L., 1877; CINCINNATI, N.L., 1878-80
BUFFALO, N.L., 1881-85; DETROIT, N.L., 1886-88
PITTSBURGH, N.L., 1889; BUFFALO, P.L., 1890
CONSUMMATE GENTLEMAN BALLPLAYER AND 19TH CENTURY STAR WHO
BATTED .312 IN 20 SEASONS, 12 TIMES HITTING .300 OR BETTER.
CONSIDERED ONE OF THE PREMIER CATCHERS OF HIS ERA BEFORE
MAKING THE TRANSITION TO STAR THIRD BASEMAN. LED TEAMS TO SIX
CHAMPIONSHIPS. RENOWNED FOR HIS INTEGRITY AND CHARACTER,
SUPERIOR SKILL AND ALL-AROUND PLAY. TWO-TIME BATTING CHAMPION.
PACED N.L. IN NEARLY EVERY OFFENSIVE CATEGORY IN 1877.
COLLECTED
THE FIRST HIT IN PROFESSIONAL BASEBALL LEAGUE HISTORY IN 1871.

DENTON TRUE "CY" YOUNG

First awarded in 1956, the Cy Young Award was Commissioner Ford Frick's method of annually recognizing the best pitcher in baseball. The previous fall, Cy Young himself had passed away on a farm where he did odd jobs, living a meager life forty-four years after having pitched in his final major league game. However, he was still so widely known as a great of the game that Frick solidified the implicit connection between Young's name and pitching greatness in a way that would forever allow fans to understand that Cy Young means the best in major league pitching, even if they did not know about Young's own career.

In looking at Cy Young's career, a single number stands out as a sign of his greatness: 511. Cy Young won 511 major league baseball games over the course of his career. Only one other pitcher, Walter Johnson, won more than 400 (417), leaving the second-place finisher almost 100 wins short of Young. No one else can claim a win total above 373, 138 wins away. Still, wins were not the means of Young's dominance but merely the result of it. Throughout his career, he featured speed, control and endurance the like of which major league baseball had never seen.

Nonetheless, Denton True "Cy" Young arose from inauspicious, almost archetypal, origins. He grew up as the eldest of five children on a family farm in Gilmore, Ohio. Denton was born just shy of two years after the end of the American Civil War, in which his father served as a Union Army private. Denton's father had also played baseball during the War, and he encouraged his sons in the game. Of course, the farm work came first, even causing Denton to leave school after completing the sixth grade. In addition to practicing his throwing during lunch breaks on the farm, Denton played baseball recreationally in Gilmore. A better pitcher than hitter, by the time Denton was seventeen, he was playing baseball on semiprofessional teams in the surrounding area. Pitching and playing second base, Denton

160

distinguished himself enough on an 1889 New Athens championship team to receive an invitation to try out for the Canton, Ohio, Tri-State League team, which is where his professional career and his legend would begin.

During his tryout for the Canton team, Cy was nervous and, while pitching, he threw the ball as hard as he could. In his own words, he "almost tore the boards off the grandstand with my fast ball." Young immediately earned the nickname Cyclone because he left the fence looking as though a cyclone had struck it. Of course, Young was signed by the Canton team (for $60 a month), and Cyclone would eventually be shortened to Cy. During the fourteen weeks of the 1890 season that Young actually pitched for Canton, his number of pitching appearances is somewhat disputed. It is clear that he collected a 15-15 record, with some accounts of him having started 29 games and relieved twice. Other accounts assert that he completed 26 games and finished ten others. In any event, he was clearly Canton's best pitcher, even in his first professional season, striking out 201 batters and walking only 33, numbers compiled only through the end of June. Cy apparently last pitched for Canton on June 25th, throwing a no-hitter with eighteen strikeouts and no walks. At that point, the major league need for pitching talent led to his purchase by the Cleveland Spiders, a team that had evolved from the American Association's Forest Citys. The Canton manager was able to demand the price he needed for his young phenom – a new suit of clothes.

Cy's rise to the majors may have been the only thing in baseball faster than his own fast ball. Because the 1890 Players' League had pulled so much talent away from the National League, he found himself making his major league debut just over a month after leaving tri-state ball, on August 6, 1890, against Chicago's Anson's Colts. He three-hit the Colts, who would eventually go on to finish in second place, and he won his debut 8-1. After the game, Cap Anson purportedly offered the Spiders $1000 for their new pitcher, an offer that they promptly declined. Cy went on to further success as the season concluded, ending up as the only winning pitcher, with a 9-7 record after winning both games of a doubleheader on the season's final day, on a poor Cleveland team that ended up in seventh place, forty-three and a half games out of first place. He finished with a 3.47 earned run average, completing all sixteen games that he started and compiling 39 strikeouts and 30 walks. In fact, Cy's base on balls per 9 innings rate was the best in the league.

1891, Young's first full major league season, opened with excitement as the Cleveland Spiders moved into newly constructed League Park, which featured 9,000 wooden seats for spectators. Young started the park's first game against the Cincinnati Reds and won 12-3. Cy would go on to post a 27-22 record for the season, completing 43 of the 46 games that he started. However, the Spiders were not able to build on his success. The team finished in fifth, twenty-two and a half games out of first place, winning only 38 games more than Young himself. During the course of the year, Cy had begun to earn some money that really allowed him to save for the first time. He was paid $1400 for his first full season with the Spiders, and according to Cy, he "got home with more than $1000 of that year's pay. And when I got home, with more money in one lump than anyone in these hills had ever seen, I married the girl on the next farm." Cy's marriage to Robba Miller actually occurred in November 1892, the most important of many important events to happen to him that year.

Cy Young, 1909-1911
T-206
Courtesy of Library of Congress PPOC

1892 was a year of achievement. Playing alongside fellow future Hall-of-Famers John Clarkson, George Davis and Jesse Burkett, Cy led the Spiders to the best season that, to that point, the team had ever had. In achieving what would have been a second place overall finish for the season, the Spiders actually achieved more because the league had agreed to a split season where the lead team of the first half would play a championship series against the lead team of the second half. After a fifth-place start in the first half, the Spiders won the second half, and they faced the Boston Beaneaters in the

National League's World Championship Series. Cy pitched three complete games in the series, the first of which ended in a tie, but the Spiders lost all of the other five games. Through they lost the series, they proved that they were a team to be taken seriously. For his part, Cy Young had established himself as a superstar. During the course of the 1892 season, he went 36-12, leading the league in victories, a 1.93 earned run average, and nine shutouts. He completed 48 of the 49 games that he started. Of course, he was married that fall, and to finish the year, he was featured in the December publication of *The Sporting News*.

Inevitably, the 1892 season, which had featured dominant pitching by Young and others, brought changes to the game. A pitching plate was installed five feet behind the distance that had previously existed for a pitching box, establishing the 60.5-foot distance from the pitching rubber to home plate. The additional five feet of distance was supposed to help to improve the game's offense, a repeat of a strategy of adjustment that had been used in 1883. The change was problematic for many major league pitchers, but Young continued his dominance. While his earned run average rose by 1.43 runs per game in 1893, the league average rose by 1.38 runs per game, so he still finished in third place overall in that category. Over the next three seasons, he posted records of 34-16 in 1893, 26-21 in 1894, and 35-10 in 1895 when he led the league in both wins and shutouts. Young attributed his continued excellence to the farm work that he did between baseball seasons and to the fact that he did not tire his arm by throwing many warm-up pitches. In fact, Young claimed never to have had a sore arm during his career, despite the fact that he averaged more than 41 complete games per season during his nine full seasons in the 1890s.

In 1895, the Cleveland Spiders managed another second-place finish, allowing them to play in the Temple Cup, or World Championship Series against the Baltimore Orioles to establish which team was the National League's best. While experimenting with a new pitch (a slow ball that would become the modern change-up) in addition to his fastball and two types of curve balls, Young won three victories against the Orioles, leading the Spiders to a 4-1 record overall in the series and their long-awaited championship.

During the 1896 season, Young led the league in shutouts and strikeouts, but more importantly, his control had manifested to the point that he had more than twice as many strikeouts to walks (140-62). In addition to completing 42 of the 46 games that he started, he also led the league in saves with three. He also posted career highs in homeruns hit (3) and runs batted in (28), though that statistic wasn't officially kept until 1920. In addition to his pitching workload, the respect he had earned also led him to act as an umpire in two games that season for which the regular umpires were unavailable. He almost achieved his first career no-hitter against the Philadelphia Phillies, only to lose it to Ed Delahanty with two outs in the

Cy Young, 1911
Turkey Red Cabinets (T3)
Courtesy of Library of Congress PPOC

ninth. A no-hitter would have to wait until September 19th of the 1897 season against the Cincinnati Reds. Young never considered the 6-0 victory to be a legitimate no-hitter because, of the game's four Spiders' errors, one was initially deemed a hit, only to be changed to an error when the Spiders' third baseman sent a note to the press box to take responsibility. Still, famously, in the words of the *Cleveland Plain Dealer*, the Reds' batters "walked up to be slaughtered only because the rules required and not for the good it did them."

In the summer of 1898, as the Spanish American War raged briefly, contributing to an ever-growing sense of American strength and empire, the Cleveland Spiders struggled with poor attendance. Young's control continued to improve, and he pitched to a 25-13 records with a 2.53 era while completing 40 of his 41 starts, and the Spiders finished in fifth place in the twelve-team league, but the team was not sustainable. At season's end, the Spiders' owners purchased the St. Louis Browns, renamed the team the

Perfectos, and transferred Cy Young and their other strong players to the Perfectos roster. In 1899, the Cleveland Spiders would post the worst win-loss percentage in baseball history, and at the end of the season, the team would be dissolved. Young spent two years in St. Louis (1899 with the Perfectos and 1900, when the team changed its name to the St. Louis Cardinals). While Young's strikeouts to walk ratio continued to improve as he led the league in complete games in 1898 and in shutouts the following season, he did not dazzle as in years past, and the St. Louis team finished in fifth place each year. Young's disappointing 19-19 record in 1900, which can perhaps be explained by league contraction, further left the baseball world wondering if twentieth century baseball had any room for Denton "Cy" Young.

To achieve a change of venue and a higher salary, Cy Young jumped to the Boston Americans of the newly formed American League in 1901. He actually waited for an extended period before signing with Boston on March 19th in order to allow St. Louis to make a competitive offer, but St. Louis determined that Young's skills were beginning to decline. Young then immediately led the American League in wins, strikeouts and earned run average, earning the unofficial triple crown of pitching. During that off-season, Cy Young, with a sixth-grade education, became a pitching coach for Harvard University. His coaching services were widely respected and, during the following off-season, Young coached at Mercer University, and that team went on to win its state championship for the next three seasons.

Young's return to dominance continued for several seasons, leading him to post win totals of 32, 28, and 26 in 1902-1904. His strikeout to walk ratio reached a career best in 1905 at 210-30, and he posted a career-best earned run average of 1.26 in 1908. The highlight of his Boston career occurred in 1903, the year when he happened to post a career high .321 batting average. In that season, Boston won the American League pennant and agreed to play the Pittsburgh Pirates in the first modern World Series between the two Major Leagues. Young threw the very first pitch in World Series history, and while he gave up four runs in his first inning of pitching, he went on to pitch in four games of the best-of-nine series, starting three, of which he won two and lost one. He also drove in three runs as he helped Boston take the series from Honus Wagner's Pirates five games to three. Boston again finished in first place during the 1904 season, but John McGraw's New York Giants refused to play against them in a World Series, so the Series was not played and Young would never reach another during his career. However, in 1953, an eighty-six-year-old Young would appear to throw the ceremonial first pitch in the World Series between the Brooklyn Dodgers and New York Yankees – a strike that was caught by a young catcher named Lawrence "Yogi" Berra.

Cy Young, 1909-1911
T-206
Courtesy of Library of Congress PPOC

Moving forward, Cy Young would repeatedly face off against a worthy rival: future Hall of Fame Philadelphia Athletics pitcher Rube Waddell. Three days after being on the losing side of a Waddell one-hitter in 1904, Young faced Waddell and the Athletics again and threw a perfect game, retiring Waddell as the final out. The game was part of a Cy Young streak that realized 45 consecutive shutout innings and 76 consecutive batters (25.1 innings) without surrendering a hit. It was also the first perfect game under baseball's modern rules. Young would go on to throw a third career no-hitter in 1908, but even he felt that his games against Waddell were more memorable. In what he called "the greatest game of ball I ever took part in," Young faced Waddell in Boston on July 4, 1905, in one of the greatest pitching showcases in baseball history. Both pitchers pitched the entirety of that contest, which lasted 20 innings, each pitcher delivering approximately 250-300 pitches. Young lost the game because his defense collapsed in the 20th inning, but he pitched 18 scoreless innings overall, including 13 consecutive scoreless innings. The *Philadelphia Inquirer* described the game as the "best performance in the history of the league." The game, by the way, was the second game of a double-header. Waddell had also pitched in the final inning of the first game to earn a save, leading him to pitch 21 overall innings. Young and Waddell would face off again in 1907 with a thirteen-inning scoreless tie. Still, Cy Young was the king of baseball pitchers, as was evidence on 1908's Cy Young Day, during which all of the all-stars from other American League teams were brought to Boston to face Young and his Red Sox, the team's name that had been newly adopted that season. While Young only pitched briefly in the game, more than 20,000 fans were on hand to watch him receive gifts between innings.

Young was traded back to Cleveland before the 1909 season, in which he would win 19 games for the Naps, which placed him fourth in the league, while completing thirty games, which found him ranked second. It was the last great season of his career. For the next two seasons, he continued to pitch for the Naps until he was released and picked up by the Boston Rustlers to finish the 1911 season. Clearly the major leagues' oldest player, in 1912, he made one more attempt with the Rustlers, and during spring training, *The Sporting News* wrote of him, "The old boy is said to look better than any previous season since 1663, considered by many to be his best years since the Summer of 1169." At the age of forty-five, while he still drew great numbers of fans, Young could no longer pitch in accordance with his own legend, and he retired in May without ever having taken the field that season. Young returned to his family farm only to return to professional baseball briefly during the 1913 season as the manager of the Federal League's Cleveland Green Sox, whom he led to second place. Young parted ways with the team when it was moved to Toronto the following year.

Even more important than Cy Young's skill and his success, though it is a by-product of both of them, Young's longevity allowed him to follow baseball in its transition to the modern era. He pitched to players, such as Cap Anson, who began professional baseball in the early 1870s, and he pitched to players, such as Eddie Collins, who carried major league baseball into the 1930s. When Young began his career, major league pitchers were still pitching underhand, and foul balls were not counted as strikes. His major league debut occurred just one year after the number of balls required for a walk was lowered to four; eight balls had been required for a walk just a decade earlier. In Young's fourth year, the pitching mound was moved back five feet from home plate, to its current distance of 60 feet, 6 inches. It was not until Young's sixth season that he began to wear a glove in the field. Baseball was changing as it matured, but Cy Young's success remained a constant.

Cy Young did not leave the game of baseball as a rich man. He would struggle financially after his retirement, playing exhibition games in his sixties during the Great Depression and taking necessary jobs as a store clerk and handyman. His only child, a daughter, died just a few hours after birth in

1907, and the death of his wife in 1933 left him dependent upon friends and former teammates for company. Still, without riches or descendants, Cy Young left a legacy that holds his name synonymous with pitching excellence more than a century after he last took the field. Appropriately, he was present for the festivities as the Major League Baseball Hall of Fame Museum was dedicated on June 12, 1939.

Major League Debut: August 6, 1890, for the Cleveland Spiders

Final Major League Game: October 11, 1911, for the Boston Rustlers

Win-loss record: 511-316

Complete Games: 749

Career Earned Run Average: 2.63

Career Strikeouts: 2,803

Pitching Triple Crown: 1901

Inducted to the Major League Baseball Hall of Fame: 1937

Young's Hall of Fame Plaque Reads:

> DENTON T. (CY) YOUNG
> CLEVELAND (N) 1890-98
> ST. LOUIS (N) 1899-1900
> BOSTON (A) 1901-08
> CLEVELAND (A) 1909-11
> BOSTON (N) 1911
> ONLY PITCHER IN FIRST HUNDRED
> YEARS OF BASEBALL TO WIN 500 GAMES.
> AMONG HIS 511 VICTORIES WERE 3
> NO-HIT SHUTOUTS, PITCHED PERFECT
> GAME MAY 5, 1904, NO OPPOSING
> BATSMAN REACHING FIRST BASE.

POST-GAME POSTSCRIPT

"Whoever wants to know the heart and mind of America had better
learn baseball." – Jacques Barzun.

Baseball is implicitly American in nature, which is not to say that the
game cannot exist and thrive elsewhere, but it is to say that the game has
grown and matured along with the United States, sharing both successes and
shortcomings. Baseball helped to install a cultural unity throughout the states
in the aftermath of the Civil War, and its popularity helped to rally urban
populations in a healthy form of competition and nationalism as the second
industrial revolution enriched and strengthened America, positioning it to
take a more bold and consequential position in global affairs in the coming
twentieth century. Through a balance reminiscent of the tensions inherent in
federalism, necessary stability was established through the relationship
between teams and the leagues in which they played. When the game was
able to bring together players of differing regions, religions and ethnicities,
providing opportunity through pursuit of a common objective while players
were valued based on their abilities and character, baseball reflected the most
important and central aspirations of the United States. However, beyond the
intertwined relationship that professional baseball has with its native country,
legitimate influence and impact also exists. In 1955, former president Herbert
Hoover was quoted as saying, "Next to religion, baseball has had a greater
impact on our American way of life than any other American institution."
President Hoover recognized the impact that baseball has beyond recreation
and entertainment. Baseball's survival as a professional sport was dependent
upon the country's technology, infrastructure and media realities, and at the
same time, the sport enabled those industries to expand, thereby providing
tangible mutual benefit.

At the same time, baseball has struggled in the ways that America
has struggled – perhaps most profoundly with race and with labor. Jackie

Robinson would not have needed to be groundbreaking if Cap Anson hadn't refused to field a team against an opponent that included African-American players. Instead, segregation of the game provided a precursor to *Plessy v. Ferguson*'s "separate but equal" language. Disagreements about players' rights, contracts and compensation created a chaotic environment in which players could jump from league to league, which resulted in considerable damage to personal and professional relationships and culminated in the brief experiment of the Players' League. Such struggles linked the experiences of professional athletes to those of the labor class as incidents such as the Homestead Strike and the Pullman Strike occurred and organizations such as the Knights of Labor and the American Federation of Labor sought to cultivate membership. As the players found that they could not operate independently of investors and organizers, American labor battled vigilantly for what concessions they could obtain.

The players highlighted in this book were a part of those times and events in baseball history; they were threads in the fabric of the game that secured it to the growth and maturation of the United States. At the same time, they were innovators and pioneers within the game of baseball itself. Baseball did not arrive to the American people as a finished product. Instead, its rules and structure have required constant attention and careful sculpting in order to maximize the game's potential in a given time and context. Field dimension, equipment innovations and basic rules changed dramatically in the late nineteenth century, and the results led only to further innovations in the twentieth century as part of baseball's seemingly endless potential for success through growth and change. At the same time, the players in this text, professional baseball's first superstars, also created statistical and performance precedents that would begin baseball's perpetual attachment to its own history. As points of comparison, to facilitate the recognition of greatness, to provide a continual narrative of the game, from professional baseball's first pitch, the players involved inherently contracted a type of immortality.

Baseball's nineteenth century players essentially fulfilled a lead off role in these fundamental aspects of the game. They didn't play for immortality, but they proved that it could be achieved. At the same time, they built a foundation upon which future generations would develop the game and the American narrative even further. The period's superstars had leverage to influence the game, and their careers and reputations permitted them a broader reach than that of most players. Still, because of the distance in time and the differences between the game they knew and what it is now, they are no longer widely known in the manner that Ruth, Cobb, Gehrig and other superstars of the early twentieth century still are today. Hopefully this text, while it only addresses eighteen such nineteenth century Hall of Famers, provides some insight into who they were as men and how they impacted the sport. While they were mere men and they carried the resulting flaws, they were each capable of utter greatness on the field that demands they be forever current in the game's memory.

In his 2014 Hall of Fame acceptance speech, MVP player and famed New York Yankees manager Joe Torre asserted, "Baseball is a game of life. It's not perfect, but it feels like it is. That's the magic of it. We are responsible for giving it the respect that it deserves. Our sport is part of the American soul, and it's ours to borrow just for a while, to take care of it for a time, and then pass it on to the next generation. When I say us, I mean as managers and players. If all of us who love baseball are doing our jobs, then those who get the game from us will be as proud to be a part of it as we were." Baseball is in continual development, and its history continues to be formed with each executed play. As those that play the game care for it before passing it on, by understanding baseball's history and players that shaped the earliest decades of professional play, fans will further appreciate the game in its present form. To respect the game, and to care for it, means to honor it in all of its stages, and of course none of the professional game that we know today would exist as we know it today without that first generation of superstars who led off in giving the game its shape.

RECOMMENDED FURTHER READING

Achorn, Edward. *Fifty-nine in '84: Old Hoss Radbourn, Barehanded Baseball & the Greatest Season a Pitcher Ever Had.* Harper Perennial, 2011.

Base Ball: A Journal of the Early Game. McFarland & Company, Inc. Volume 1 (2007) – Present.

The Baseball Research Journal. Society for American Baseball Research. Volume 1 (1972) – Present.

Chadwick, Henry. *Haney's Base Ball Book of Reference.* Haney & Co., Publishers, 1867. Reprinted by Applewood Books.

Corcoran, Dennis. *Induction Day at Cooperstown: A History of the Baseball Hall of Fame Ceremony.* McFarland, 2010.

Felber, Bill. *A Game of Brawl: The Orioles, the Beaneaters, and the Battle for the 1897 Pennant.* Univ. of Nebraska Press, 2007.

Fleitz, David L. *Ghosts in the Gallery at Cooperstown: Sixteen Little-Known Members of the Hall of Fame.* McFarland, 2004.

Frommer, Harvey. *Old-Time Baseball: America's Pastime in the Gilded Age.* Lanham: Taylor Trade Publishing, 2006.

Gorman, Robert M. and David Weeks. *Death at the Ballpark: More Than 2,000 Game-Related Fatalities of Players, Other Personnel and Spectators in Amateur and Professional Baseball, 1862-2014.* McFarland, 2015.

Helyar, John. *Lords of the Realm: The Real History of Baseball.* Ballantine Books, 1994.

Henderson, Robert. *Ball, Bat and Bishop: The Origin of Ball Games.* Univ. of Illinois Press, 2001.

Inventing Baseball: The 100 Greatest Games of the Nineteenth Century. Edited by Bill Felber, SABR Nineteenth Century Committee. Society for American Baseball Research, Inc., 2013.

Kerr, Roy. *Big Dan Brouthers: Baseball's First Great Slugger.* McFarland, 2013.

Kerr, Roy. *Buck Ewing: A Baseball Biography.* McFarland, 2012.

Kirsch, George B. *Baseball in Blue and Gray: The National Pastime During the Civil War.* Princeton University Press, 2007.

Leventhal, Josh. *A History of Baseball in 100 Objects.* New York: Black Dog & Leventhal Publishers, 2015.

Millen, Patricia. *From Pastime to Passion: Baseball and the Civil War.* Heritage Books, 2001.

Ritter, Lawrence S. *The Glory of Their Times: The Story of the Early Days of Baseball Told by the Men Who Played It.* Harper Perennial Modern Classics, 2010.

Seymour, Harold. *Baseball: The Early Years.* Oxford Univ. Press, 1989.

Sowell, Mike. *July 2, 1903: The Mysterious Death of Hall-of-Famer Big Ed Delahanty.* Macmillan Pub. Co., 1902.

Spalding, Al. *America's National Game.* American Sports Publishing Co., 1911.

Thorn, John. *Baseball in the Garden of Eden: The Secret History of the Early Game.* New York: Simon & Schuster, 2011.

Several websites and online databases were also of great use in the researching of the book. The National Baseball Hall of Fame website was a great resource, as was Baseball-Reference.com, a treasure-trove of statistics and seasonal rankings dating back well into the nineteenth century. The Society for American Baseball Research, or SABR, also features an incredible website with extensively researched, detailed articles covering the lives and careers of nineteenth century baseball players, among others.

This work does not proport to offer groundbreaking research, but instead intends to connect established research accessible to those who are not familiar with it and to, when appropriate, place key moments of baseball's history into the appropriate context of United States history. Doing so allows for the themes of race, labor relations, and urbanization, among others, to be more fully appreciated.

For students of history and baseball enthusiasts, the works referenced above represent only a portion of the wealth of knowledge to which we are fortunate to have access. Doubtless, future research and publication will do even more to uncover the story of the development of America's national pastime.

About the Author:

A native of Hattiesburg, MS, Ray Scheetz is an avid baseball fan and history teacher who lives in the Nashville, TN, area with his wife and two children.